DATA VISUALIZATIONS AND INFOGRAPHICS

Library Technology Essentials

About the Series

The *Library Technology Essentials* series helps librarians utilize today's hottest new technologies as well as ready themselves for tomorrow's. The series features titles that cover the A–Z of how to leverage the latest and most cutting-edge technologies and trends to deliver new library services.

Today's forward-thinking libraries are responding to changes in information consumption, new technological advancements, and growing user expectations by devising groundbreaking ways to remain relevant in a rapidly changing digital world. This collection of primers guides libraries along the path to innovation through step-by-step instruction. Written by the field's top experts, these handbooks serve as the ultimate gateway to the newest and most promising emerging technology trends. Filled with practical advice and projects for libraries to implement right now, these books inspire readers to start leveraging these new techniques and tools today.

About the Series Editor

Ellyssa Kroski is the Director of Information Technology at the New York Law Institute as well as an award-winning editor and author of 22 books including *Law Librarianship in the Digital Age* for which she won the AALL's 2014 Joseph L. Andrews Legal Literature Award. Her ten-book technology series, The Tech Set, won the ALA's Best Book in Library Literature Award in 2011. She is a librarian, an adjunct faculty member at Pratt Institute, and an international conference speaker. She speaks at several conferences a year, mainly about new tech trends, digital strategy, and libraries.

Titles in the Series

DATA VISUALIZATIONS AND INFOGRAPHICS

Sarah K. C. Mauldin

ROWMAN & LITTLEFIELD
Lanham • Boulder • New York • London

Published by Rowman & Littlefield
A wholly owned subsidiary of The Rowman & Littlefield Publishing Group, Inc.
4501 Forbes Boulevard, Suite 200, Lanham, Maryland 20706
www.rowman.com

Unit A, Whitacre Mews, 26-34 Stannary Street, London SE11 4AB

British Library Cataloguing in Publication Information Available

Library of Congress Cataloging-in-Publication Data

Mauldin, Sarah K. C., 1977-
Data visualizations and infographics / Sarah K.C. Mauldin.
p. cm.
Includes bibliographical references and index.
ISBN 978-1-4422-4386-6 (cloth : alk. paper) – ISBN 978-1-4422-4387-3 (pbk. : alk. paper) – ISBN 978-1-4422-4388-0 (ebook)
1. Library science–Graphic methods. 2. Charts, diagrams, etc.–Design. 3. Communication in library science. 4. Visual communication. 5. Information visualization. I. Title.
Z678.93.G73M38 2015
020.22'2–dc23
2015011707

♾ ™ The paper used in this publication meets the minimum requirements of American National Standard for Information Sciences Permanence of Paper for Printed Library Materials, ANSI/NISO Z39.48-1992.

Printed in the United States of America

CONTENTS

SERIES EDITOR'S FOREWORD

Data Visualizations and Infographics is a start-to-finish induction into how to display data through the creation of engaging and effective visual representations. Expert author Sarah Mauldin provides a comprehensive overview of the landscape of free and low-cost data visualization and infographics tools, professional services available, and data sources to fuel your creations. She walks readers through how to use cutting-edge applications to keep patrons informed, market the library, and build community. This complete field guide covers everything from using common tools such as Microsoft Word and PowerPoint to create infographics to how to mindmap brainstorming meetings, create stellar interactive maps with imported data, design website flowcharts and diagrams, develop interactive timelines, and create instructional infographics with tools such as Piktochart, Easel.ly, Creately, and more.

The idea for the Library Technology Essentials book series came about because there have been many drastic changes in information consumption, new technological advancements, and growing user expectations over the past few years that forward-thinking libraries are responding to by devising groundbreaking ways to remain relevant in a rapidly changing digital world. I saw a need for a practical set of guidebooks that libraries could use to inform themselves about how to stay on the cutting edge by implementing new programs, services, and technologies to match their patrons' expectations.

Libraries today are embracing new and emerging technologies, transforming themselves into community hubs and places of co-creation through makerspaces, developing information commons spaces, and even taking on new roles and formats, all the while searching for ways to decrease budget lines, add value, and prove the ROI of the library. The Library Technology Essentials series is a collection of primers to guide libraries along the path to innovation through step-by-step instruction. Written by the field's top experts, these handbooks are meant to serve as the ultimate gateway to the newest and most promising emerging technology trends. Filled with practical advice and project ideas for libraries to implement right now, these books will hopefully inspire readers to start leveraging these new techniques and tools today.

Each book follows the same format and outline, guiding the reader through the A–Z of how to leverage the latest and most cutting-edge technologies and trends to deliver new library services. The "Projects" chapter comprises the largest portion of the books, providing library initiatives that can be implemented by both beginner and advanced readers, accommodating for all audiences and levels of technical expertise. These projects and programs range from the basic "How to Circulate Wearable Technology in Your Library" and "How to Host a FIRST Robotics Team at the Library" to intermediate such as "How to Create a Hands-Free Digital Exhibit Showcase with Microsoft Kinect" to the more advanced options such as "Implementing a Scalable E-Resources Management System" and "How to Gamify Library Orientation for Patrons with a Top Down Video Game." Readers of all skill levels will find something of interest in these books.

I had the pleasure of working with Sarah Mauldin on a previous book through which I learned that she was an exceptional writer and information professional. Sarah was named an Emerging Leader by the AALL (American Association of Law Libraries) in 2010 and rightly so; she has been a very active innovator in the field serving in local and national leadership roles in various library professional associations. I knew that she would bring her extensive knowledge and expertise to this book and she did just that. Sarah has put together an outstanding guide to creating infographics and data visualizations in libraries. If you're thinking about how you can utilize these new visual tools for your library, this is the book for you.

—Ellyssa Kroski
Director of Information Technology
The New York Law Institute

http://www.ellyssakroski.com
http://ccgclibraries.com
ellyssakroski@yahoo.com

PREFACE

Data Visualizations and Infographics is, above all, a how-to-do-it book. It is also a when-to-do-it and why-to-do-it book but its real purpose is to provide you with the tools and inspiration you need to use infographics and data visualization techniques in your library, no matter what setting you find yourself in. I hope you will find the power within this volume to try something new and knock your audience's socks off as you tell your story in a visual format that can be consumed and understood at a glance.

The majority of the examples you will find in this book are designed with public and academic librarians in mind, but the techniques and tools are just as applicable to archivists, school librarians, and special librarians of all kinds. The following chapters are a starting point to get your creative juices flowing as you see all of the ways these tools can and have been used to great advantage by librarians and information professionals in many settings and for many purposes.

The book begins with a brief introduction, including a short history of infographics and some ideas about how this book can help you become a visualization expert. Next is a chapter describing what you need to get started, how to determine if an infographic or data visualization is the right vehicle for the story you have in mind, and a very brief overview of the tools available. Next you will find an in-depth look at the tools discussed in this book as well as an overview of some of the many sources of public and free information available to help you craft your story. Once you are familiar with the tools you can see how librarians in many different settings have used infographics and data visualizations to aid in teaching, to share large amounts of data in an easy-to-use format, to show what the library can do, and many other innovative and beautiful projects. Then each of the tools described is used in a real world scenario that you can follow along with as you start exploring the free and low-cost development resources available online. Next you can get a taste of tips, tricks, and best practices for making your project a success and also see what the future may hold for this rapidly expanding format for information delivery. Finally there is an annotated list of recommended resources to help you explore the visualization field in more depth and gain inspiration and ideas from bloggers and others who are using these tools every day.

There is no right way to use this book. You can start at the beginning and read it cover to cover or use the table of contents as a guide to the exact tool or concept you need now. You can also flip through the book seeking inspiration and enjoying the artistry of the case study graphics or zero in on a particular tool or step-by-step example and dive right in to your first project. However you choose to use this book remember that the examples provided are only examples and that you can build on them in whatever way you see fit to create amazing and astounding visualizations and infographics of your own. I would love to see some of the great things you design while you tell your library's story, so feel free to share.

ACKNOWLEDGMENTS

This, I am overwhelmingly proud to say, is my first book. Doesn't that just sound wonderful as you read it in your head? Please take this as inspiration that you too can do something for publication, whether it's a short article for a community organization newsletter, a thesis or dissertation, a poetry chapbook, a letter to the editor, a work of fiction, a book chapter, or even a full-blown book. Most people who have picked up this book and are currently reading the acknowledgments already make a living around words, so I challenge each of you to write something and to remember that it can be oh so much more fun to do something because it is hard and not just because you can toss it off in the time it takes you to read this. You picked up this book to, I hope, do something amazing with it and I think that puts you comfortably within the ranks of the awesome. Keep it up and I can't wait to see you in an OPAC somewhere, gentle reader.

A book does not come about all by itself. This one started with Ellyssa Kroski, a series editor with the idea for the twelve books in this collection. She sought authors and somehow decided I might be good at this. I thought I might, too, but quickly learned that a job and a house and a husband can be detrimental to our best intentions and plans. I thank Ellyssa dearly for her guidance, encouragement, advice, and pleasant habit of being in New York while I was in Georgia, making it somewhat difficult to strangle me for making things difficult. However, I believe that the better angels of her nature are somewhat less than homicidal, so I was probably safe at any rate. Thanks again for giving me a few chances and I hope I showed you that sheer cussed meanness can go a very long way.

Now, on to those who had parts, no matter how small, in making this book a reality. I thank those who were so very generous with their time and talents in the Case Studies chapter, including: Mary Kay Jung and the staff of the Thompson Coburn LLP Library; Courtney Drysdale, Public Services Librarian at RMC Health; Liz Johns, Librarian for Education, Johns Hopkins University; Emily Cunningham Rushing, Competitive Intelligence Manager at Haynes & Boone, Jennifer S. Swanson, Senior Market Analyst at Draper Laboratories; Chris Olson of Chris Olson & Associates, Drew Lichtenstein, Senior Content Developer at HarvardX; Melissa D'Agostino, Instruction Librarian, Cecil College; Kimberly Miller, Research and Instrction Librarian, Towson University; Seth Allen, Online Instruction Librarian, King University; Ashley Moye, Metadata & Digital Initiatives Librarian, Charlotte School of Law; and Rachel Langlois, Virtual Services Librarian, New Hanover County Public Library, Wilmington, NC as well as Library Director Harry Tuchmayer and Assistant Director Paige Owens for getting us together. I also thank everyone I chatted with, asked questions of, or generally bothered about this whether I was together enough to remember your name at the time or not.

A special thanks to Xeno and Harry, best and most awesome respectively, who never can understand why there is a computer in my lap and not one (or both) of them or when sitting at a table find it a joy to cover some useful computer keys or notes or anything else with some part of their anatomies. You are both perfect companions.

Last, but never least, I thank my husband, Ryan, who has been very nice about the piles of books, my somewhat fanciful goals for what I could do in a day, and the constantly open laptop. Forever and a day, even if I'm providing my own charts and graphs.

I

AN INTRODUCTION TO DATA VISUALIZATIONS AND INFOGRAPHICS

The greatest value of a picture is when it forces us to notice what we never expected to see.—John W. Tukey, *Exploratory Data Analysis* (Reading, Mass.: Addison-Wesley, 1977), vi.

Why should you, an information professional, be interested in the content of this book? The short answer is in the word information. Whatever you may call your position (librarian, analyst, info pro, curator, archivist, etc.) and in whatever setting you work, you most assuredly do that work with information. This book is about corralling information of all shapes, sizes, and types into manageable and readable presentations that can be easily comprehended by management, colleagues, patrons, or anyone else who may want or need to see the data but are pressed for time and attention. Infographics and data visualizations make enormous spreadsheets and piles of statistics far friendlier to the average user. This makes users happy and provides librarians the chance to look amazing by taking dry and dull statistics and turning them into beautiful, colorful, and meaningful charts and graphics. Be ready to wow your organization with this newfound ability to transform what was once boring into something awesome.

WHAT ARE INFOGRAPHICS?

Infographics, at the most basic level, are two-dimensional images that represent or convey information in an easily understandable form. The *Oxford English Dictionary* cites a 1979 quotation from Eric de Grolier[1] as the first use of the term in print. Infographics have since been embraced by newspapers, often appearing as "Snapshots" on the front page of *USA Today*[2] or as graphical representations included to aid reader understanding of an investigative or other long form story, as in an investigative piece by the *Atlanta Journal-Constitution* on the purchase of surplus military equipment by local governments in Georgia.[3]

Infographics are by no means restricted to the pages of newspapers. Many magazines, notably *WIRED*, here using graphics and visualizations to explain a recent rain event in Southern California,[4] *Mental Floss* with Miss Kathleen's *The Great Library Stereotypometer*,[5] and *Fast Company* using a *New York Times* infographic showing the decline of men in the American workforce as its Infographic of the Day,[6] have adopted them as a content staple. And it isn't just print media that has embraced the visual display of information. Government agencies, universities, companies, individuals, and many more have also started creating infographics for serious business, like showing the dangers of smoking[7] or population trends[8] and for the far less, to some, serious business of the Evolution of Star Trek[9] or a chart of super powers sorted by type of power.[10]

A SHORT HISTORY OF INFOGRAPHICS

As noted above, infographics are nothing more than visual representations of data and other information. This clouds the definition somewhat as we consider that people have been sharing information with others through pictures since at least the time that Paleolithic humans made rudimentary paintings of animals, both good to eat and good to avoid, with simple tools in caves at Lascaux, France. People continued to create all kinds of graphics, including timelines, diagrams, charts, maps, and graphs that helped others understand mathematical concepts, human anatomy, and many other ideas that might be difficult to

"Lascaux II" by Jack Versloot—originally posted to Flickr as Lascaux II. *Licensed under CC BY 2.0 via Wikimedia Commons—http://commons.wikimedia.org/wiki/ File:Lascaux_II.jpg#mediaviewer/File:Lascaux_II.jpg, http://tinyurl.com/kvr984j, accessed March 3, 2015.*

visualize. This has continued, with ever easier-to-use tools, up to the present day.

In the twentieth century, magazines and newspapers started to become more visual and moved away from simple columns of text. Photojournalism became a recognized form since the early twentieth century, with the first Pulitzer Prize for Photography given in 1942 and the award changed to Feature Photography in 1968 and a new category for Breaking News Photography added in 2000.[11] As more and more publications began printing in full color, pictures became more and more expected. The advent of the infographic added even more to print and then online journalism. While a photograph can tell a powerful story, an infographic provides context and information, often in a truly beautiful package. The rise of online journalism added the ability for these picture stories to use interactive elements, making them ever-more-powerful tools for telling a story, whether deeply serious or pointedly frivolous. While there is no Pulitzer for infographic and data visualization

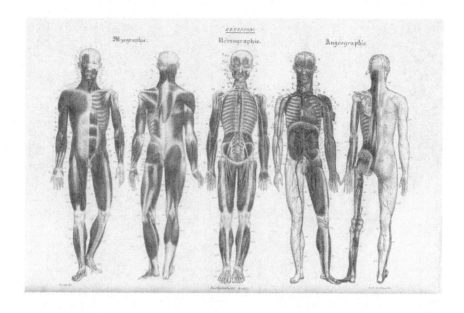

From Jean-Baptiste Sarlandière, illustrated by Louis Courtin. *Anatomie métho-dique, ou Organographie humaine en tableaux synoptiques, avec figures. A l'usage des universités, pour les facultés et écoles de médecine et de chirurgie, les acadé-mies de peinture et de sculpture, et les collèges royaux. Source: Paris: Chez les libraires de médecine et chez l'auteur, 1829, plate 15 from the collection of the Nation-al Library of Medicine Historical Anatomies on the Web, http://tinyurl.com/9bzlve, ac-cessed December 24, 2014.*

yet, perhaps it is on the horizon, waiting for you, the citizen journalists and visual storytellers working with the tools and techniques that follow.

VISUALIZING DATA

Data comes in many forms, and the development of computers from the room-sized ENIAC, built strictly for computation tasks, to the modern graphics-enabled computer that sits on a desk or even in your pocket, has made it possible to take visualization and manipulation of that data beyond bar charts and scatter plots and into a new world of three-dimensional and manipulable information that can bring sense and understanding to the flood of data points that can now be comfortably carried on a flash drive. Stephen Few, in *Now You See It*,[12] his 2009 book on data visualization, quotes Card, Mackinlay, and Shneiderman[13] for the definition of what they call information visualization. "Their definition features the following characteristics: Computer-supported . . . Interactive . . . Visual representations . . . Abstract data . . . Amplify cognition. . . . All of these characteristics are important to the definition, but none more so than the last: amplifying cognition. The purpose of information visualization is not to make pictures, but to help us think."

Data visualizations are most often used in scientific disciplines to make sense of large quantities of data or to model scenarios that might be at work but invisible owing to outlying data points. Although you might not have a need to model complex weather data over centuries, you most likely do need to be able to create and defend a budget. To do this you might want to create visualizations of different scenarios or show the budget trends in your library versus those in population growth in your area or in the budgets of other institutions of similar size in your local area, state, or nationwide.

WHAT TO EXPECT

Now that you've made it through the full introduction, you win a little preview of what you can expect to gain from this book. First, you will see an overview of infographics and visualizations with some explanation about why you might want to take the time to do any of this. Then we move on to an overview of tools for creating these pretty pictures and sources of information that can help you get started. You will get a chance to read case studies of libraries and librarians who have been successful in creating graphics and visualizations that have worked where they do and some that are award winning. Next are sample step-by-step projects using just a few of the huge number of free and fee tools available online. Then we will look at some tips and tricks to help you create something that works in your setting and that you can be proud of. Finally there is a short discussion of where infographics and data visualizations are headed and the trends in tools and techniques and, of course, an annotated bibliography with recommended books, articles, websites, and presentations you may want to look to for inspiration and guidance.

I hope that you are ready to learn a bit and step, if only just a little, into the unknown. Remember that you know more about your library, what it needs, and what your patrons want than anyone else does. Be bold and try something new. Don't worry about your drawing or graphic design skills. Those will be taken care of with the intuitive and easy-to-use tools you will learn about soon. Know that you can take your own knowledge and skills, combine them with new tools and inspiration, and make something awesome. Have fun!

NOTES

N.B.—All infographics discussed in this introductory chapter can be viewed online. Please see the endnotes for the associated URLs.

1. Eric de Grolier, *Organization of Information Systems for Government & Public Administration* (Paris: UNESCO, 1979), 38, http://tinyurl.com/pxhvjkm, accessed December 24, 2014.

2. See http://tinyurl.com/ozc2ygt, accessed December 14, 2014.

3. http://tinyurl.com/m563kuo, accessed December 14, 2014.

4. See http://tinyurl.com/n49hwsl, accessed December 14, 2014.

5. See http://tinyurl.com/ndwved8, accessed December 14, 2014.

6. See http://tinyurl.com/nk9oa4c, accessed December 14, 2014.

7. See Fume Leads to Death, http://tinyurl.com/pty5r2d, accessed December 18, 2014.

8. See http://tinyurl.com/p6k3mpy, accessed December 18, 2014.

9. See http://tinyurl.com/3tlhnwe, accessed December 18, 2014.

10. See http://tinyurl.com/3vequxa, accessed December 18, 2014.

11. The Pulitzer Prizes, "Past Winners and Finalists by Category," http://www.pulitzer.org/bycat, accessed December 14, 2014.

12. Stephen Few, *Now You See It: Simple Visualization Techniques for Quantitative Analysis* (Oakland, CA: Analytics Press, 2009), 13.

13. Stuart K. Card, Jock Mackinlay, and Ben Shneiderman, *Readings in Information Visualization: Using Vision to Think* (San Diego, CA: Academic Press, 1999), 7.

2

GETTING STARTED WITH DATA VISUALIZATIONS AND INFOGRAPHICS

SO WHAT?

Why are you reading this book? Most likely you have decided that data visualizations or infographics are at least cool or interesting and that you would like to give them a try. That is an excellent reason but that cannot be the only one. You have to decide if they are the vehicle you need to best capture the attention and spur some action on the part of your audience, whether that audience is other library staff, patrons, a board of trustees, grant-making bodies or other funders, your boss, or perhaps colleagues at a conference presentation or other educational setting.

John Emerson is a designer and graphic artist who owns a public interest consultancy called Backspace.[1] In his career Emerson has created designs, infographics, and data visualizations for corporations and large nonprofits like Amnesty International USA and the United Nations. He now works full time using his designs for advocacy in the United States and all over the world. Taking a moment to visit his webpage and look at his designs and read his writings can help you to understand how your library can use the tools you will learn in this book as advocacy tools. Everyone who reads this may have a different set of issues that they need to advocate for, but the basic principles remain the same. If you are a public librarian you may be advocating for funding at the local, state, or national level, or you may be hoping to convince patrons that a new program would be enjoyable, or that newcomers to town should visit and get a library card. If you work for a university, you may have similar funding concerns that need to be presented to those with the power of the purse, or you might be working to convince students and faculty to use new services or remember the ones already in place. For corporate and other special librarians, the needs for advocacy are almost always for funding or even continued existence as a library or may be helping to market the services of the library as a traditional source for information but also as a center for sophisticated data design, business development, and value addition. Regardless of where you work or what you do, you can always use these tools to advocate for a cause that means something to you.

DECIDING IF DATA VISUALIZATIONS AND INFOGRAPHICS ARE A GOOD FIT FOR YOU AND YOUR LIBRARY

Graphics and visualizations are powerful tools for telling a story. This story can be persuasive, asking funders like a board of trustees or a foundation for additional funding to do something new in your library or explaining how the patron base in your library has changed and that you need to change how something is done. The story may also be explanatory or meant for marketing. This will use your graphic as a tool for showing what you have already done and what you plan to do to provide even better service, programming, or whatever else you envision. This kind of story may be a part of an annual report or, like one of the case studies to come, a National Library Week piece showing law firm library patrons just what the library has done and can do. Your story may also be educational and meant specifically for patrons. It might be about how to get a library card, the history of your institution, or something else that is meaningful for your library. You may also think of other stories you want to tell beyond these. Think of the visualization of information as a sandbox that you can play in and use to develop ways of communicating with all of your audiences, whether students, lawyers, scientists, medical staff, the public, those who fund your library, directly or indirectly, or anyone else you consider important for your library to communicate with.

Given the story ideas above, the first question to ask yourself is, "What story am I trying to tell?" Next, consider who it is that the story is meant to impact, otherwise known as the audience. Third, think about how this story has been told in the past and whether that worked well or could be improved. Fourth, think about the data points you have available and what might need to be gathered to tell your story in an effective manner. Fifth, consider how much time you have to create this visual representation of your story. Sixth, what skills do you and your colleagues already possess? Are you all computer whizzes who can pick up a new software package and understand it quickly, are you comfortable using Microsoft Office, or do you need assistance using some more complicated programs but are happy with a web interface with a good FAQ or Help menu? Finally, do you have money to spend on technology like software packages or do you need to get by on a shoestring, perhaps with only the money to spend on a few color printouts?

All of these considerations should go into your decision making process. Let's try a few scenarios.

SCENARIO I—TIME, LITTLE MONEY, SKILL, LOTS OF DATA

In the first scenario, the story is a presentation to your city council about raising funding for the coming fiscal year. You have a pretty good amount of time, you are comfortable with using a computer, including using Excel for data analysis, and you have some data that you have collected about circulation statistics, patron requests for books the library doesn't have, and the salary of all staff members.

Should You Do It?

This scenario looks custom-made for a data visualization. In past years you have always provided your budget information and requests in a notebook full of spreadsheets and prose. This year you can wow your city council with an attractive graphic or data visualization that provides year-over-year comparisons of how many books and other materials have been checked out, how many requests you were unable to fill, and the stagnation of staff salaries. Your skill with Excel means that you can do the whole project using Microsoft Office, creating your final graphics in Word or PowerPoint, depending on your comfort level.

Because you have time, you have the luxury of collecting a bit more information to make the impact you want with the story of your little-library-that-could. Perhaps you should put out some comment cards and ask patrons to tell you what they like about the library and what they think could be improved, and then pepper these quotes in your graphics. Find salary surveys and any other information about what library staff in comparable areas and in comparable positions earn, and try to make your case visually for raises or other perks to retain good people. You can also break out your data and make it local to each branch, depending on how this helps or hurts the story. This next bit is very important: Don't lie with your data but also don't pepper it with red flags needlessly. If the flag is red enough it will stand out on its own and needs no help from you.

Plug all of your budget and other data into Excel and get started manipulating it with the table tools. This creates attractive and colorful charts to plug into your graphic. Once you've created a great story, prepare it as a presentation for the city council along with your budget spreadsheets and prose explanations. Most likely the council will be glad they got a break from the dryness of other city departments' requests, and your creativity on a shoestring, using only the materials at hand, will get the library noticed and better funded. How cool is that?

SCENARIO 2—A LITTLE TIME, EXPLAINING NEW SYSTEMS, NON-ENGLISH SPEAKERS

This second scenario finds you with just a few weeks before students arrive for a new fall semester and the system for entering the library, logging on to computers, and checking out materials has changed dramatically from last year. You have been tasked with providing some sort of instruction for students and faculty to navigate these new systems, partly because you helped to design them. You are also a computer whiz. To add an interesting twist, your school hosts many exchange students who are not native English speakers but who do use the library regularly.

Should You Do It?

This is a great place to use infographics because they can convey a large amount of information with few or no words. This is a plus because many of the people you are trying to instruct may have trouble with signs full of words, especially if they are unfamiliar, often the case with new technology.

To start your project you will need to gather your data. In this case it will most likely be a determination of how many infographics you will need to create based on the number of places where the systems have changed. Then you might want to come up with a standard vocabulary that will be common to all of the graphics. Finally, before you begin, consider the ways that you could design for your data and try them out on a few people who are unfamiliar with the new systems. This will help you gain perspective as the user and not as an implementer.

Once you've done all of that, your savvy computer skills let you use any of the tools that will be discussed later in this book, either as the free versions or the versions priced for educational use. If you use the pay versions, you have many more choices for graphics files, uploads, and templates to create your educational masterpieces. You can even use a product you already know well, like Microsoft Word, to create quick and easy designs.

SCENARIO 3—TIMID COMPUTER USER, COMPANY HISTORY, LITTLE TIME, WORKING ALONE

In this third scenario, you are a relatively uncomfortable computer user not asked to do much beyond typing, but definitely eager to learn anything you can. You've been asked to create a display about the history of the company you work for and need to have it done next week. You have a budget but will be working on this project alone.

Should You Do It?

Yes and no. Yes because there are some very easy-to-use free timeline products available online. No because time is short and you are somewhat afraid of trying new things online. Even that easy-to-use online timeline creator requires the use of a spreadsheet that has very specific fields that have to remain just-so to work. Your display can and should be highly graphical with historical photographs, captions, and maybe even a timeline made with software you already feel comfortable with. However, just because this project isn't the right one for an infographic or data visualization, by no means should you avoid taking the time to learn how to create these great conveyers of knowledge.

WHAT ABOUT ME? I'M A _____.

No matter which scenario describes you or your place of work, remember that any one of the above can change. You may suddenly have no time and no budget, or lots of time but no information, or lots of time and lots of budget, as unlikely as that may be. Anyone can learn to use data visualizations and infographics. It may require an expenditure of your own time and money or you may be asked to learn, complete with a workshop or other support. However it comes to be, these graphics, whether informative, funny, serious, or silly, are most definitely a part of the American landscape online and in print and are fun to create and even more fun for your patrons to absorb information from.

THE TOOLS: MAIN FEATURES AND FUNCTIONALITY

Tools for creating professional looking infographics and data visualizations have proliferated online in recent years. Some of the most commonly used are Easel.ly, Creately, Info.gram, and Piktochart for infographics. For data visualization the more common tools are Tableau Public, Mapbox, Panopticon, TIBCO Spotfire, and Cognos.

Infographic tools come in two main flavors: those that require a subscription and those that are free. Often these are the same products with different feature levels based on the pricing model you choose. In general these tools all provide a selection of templates to get you started and an online editor that gives you the opportunity to change the provided templates in any way you want. These tools also provide a blank template and the same editing tools for a truly custom product. The editors are all variations on the kind of drawing and text tools available in Microsoft Word with the functionality of chart creation from Excel all in one tidy package. Knowing this can give you confidence as you start out on your own.

A great strength of infographic tools is that they provide galleries of example graphics created by other users and professional designers. These galleries are awe inspiring and can help you feel like you really have the skill to create your own, even if you have never done it before, kind of a "that bright person did this with this tool, I'm a bright person, that means I can use this tool to make something great as well," feeling.

Infographic tools are also pleasant to use because you see the changes you've made to your template in real time and have the option to go back and change what you have done before you publish. Depending on the tool and the subscription model, you have quite a bit of control over what your output will look like. Most tools provide the option to download your graphic as a JPEG, PDF, or PNG file or give you the code needed to embed your graphic on a website. If you choose the free versions of these tools, your download choices may be more limited and may include a watermark or other symbol showing the tool used to create the graphic.

Data visualization tools also come in various flavors, with both free and subscription models as well as full-featured free trials. They work in much the same way as infographic tools but often require that the data to be visualized be imported using a spreadsheet format like XLS or CSV. Once you have imported the data you can then manipulate it using dashboards and drag-and-drop tools. Online data visualization tools are easy to use and create a very slick finished product. Depending on the package you choose, you can even create a visualization that can be modified on the fly to show time progressions, variable changes, or even how data is affected by various scenarios.

The many online tools available make it easy for anyone to be a graphic designer. It is important to remember, however, that choosing the right tool for the right project is key. Most libraries will find infographics to be more meaningful to their audiences in most situations. But that doesn't mean that you should ignore data visualization. It is a powerful tool for dealing with volumes of information that you might find in your budget, circulation and reference statistics, or the changing demographics of your city, student body, or the neighborhoods where you have branches. All of the tools we use are in some ways like chainsaws. To cut down a sixty-foot oak, a chainsaw is the right choice, but probably isn't advisable when you want to prune a small shrub. Similarly, if you choose to use that chainsaw and don't know how, someone might get hurt, while in trained hands the chainsaw brings down the tree effortlessly. The same is true with technology. Choose the right tool for the job at hand and learn to use that tool well and you will create an outstanding finished product.

HOW TO START CREATING YOUR OWN

Below you will see one of my favorite infographics of all time. It shows that the process of getting a bill through the U.S. Congress to become a law is somewhat more complicated than Schoolhouse Rock made it out to be. The graphic itself is beautiful, with the rich yellow background, the saturated colors marking the many steps, the board game path the bill can follow, and the dignified upper-right corner that quotes the

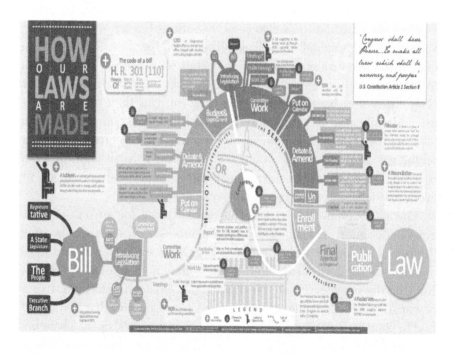

How Our Laws Are Made. *Mike Wirth Creative Commons by Attributions 3.0 at http:// tinyurl.com/lzxkyf3, accessed May 20, 2015.*

Constitution giving Congress the power to "make all laws that shall be necessary and proper." It also has other great features like textboxes that describe the possible steps a bill may go through and a legend to help the viewer understand the process. Take a moment to just look and see all of the elements. This infographic was made by someone who knew the subject matter well and had great command of color and design. That person can be you if you take the time to learn the tools and think creatively about what you know very well.

A FAILURE TO PLAN . . .

Nearly everyone reading this knows what comes after the ellipsis in the header above.[2] I don't want anyone reading this to think for a moment that anyone wants you to fail, but to succeed in the venture of infographic and data visualization creation you do have to plan, plan, and plan some more.

Before anything else, decide what story you are telling. Is it about the library, or your community, or your company, or your students, or is it about something you think is really interesting, like the legislative process you just saw? Whatever that story is, take a few minutes and flesh it out. What do you already know about it and what will you need to research? Why does it need to be told? Are you telling it because you have been told to, or do you want to tell it because it is so interesting? Who will it be shared with? What does your audience want to know and how do they want to learn it?

Now that you have thought through the story, think about time and money. Is there a budget for this project? If so how much, or how little? What about time? Did you get this project at 5:00 p.m. on a Tuesday and need to present it at 9:00 a.m. on Thursday that same week, or do you have a full semester to create something? All of these factors will have a bearing on what you plan to do.

The last part of this planning stage is figuring out what format you want. But first you need to decide what it is you are going to produce. Is your story something that should be shown as a data visualization (or even a series of visualizations)? Is it well-suited to be an infographic? Or would it be better told in prose or as a bulletin board or other display? These fun new tools are not made for every story. Trying to smash a history of your town into an infographic will most likely only make you frustrated. Also, trying to learn new software when you have a time crunch deadline will probably make you even more frustrated. Choose the right tool for the right job.

CHOOSING THE RIGHT TOOL

Now you have a plan, perhaps even a nice sketch of what you want your finished product to look like, and you are ready to get started. But where? The next thing to do is choose a tool. Have you chosen an infographic? If you are time strapped, using Microsoft Word or Power-Point might be a good idea because they are familiar and already sitting on your desktop. If you have a bit of time, you might consider trying out your design in a few of the tools described in the Step-by-Step Projects chapter to see what best suits your style and seems most comfortable. With some budget you might even try a month or two of paid subscription on a tool you like.

A version of an infographic that you might want to try is a timeline. You could create one using what is already on your desktop or use one of the tools described in Step-by-Step Projects. Both are free but they have completely different interfaces so TimelineJS and Capzles are definitely tools to try out before you decide on one.

Other specialized versions of an infographic are maps. To create these a tool is required, unless you have very advanced skills in Excel. The two discussed in the Step-by-Step Projects chapter, StatPlanet and DataFerrett, are also easy to use but, as always, it's a good idea to take the time to play with them to determine which one feels best to you.

The world of packages for data visualization may seem overwhelming. Tableau Public and Mapbox are described in Step-by-Step Projects, but there are many more available online at all price points. This is another project type where a tool is required unless your skills in Excel are very advanced or you have access to an advanced data modeling package like SPSS.

I FOUND A TOOL, WHAT NOW?

Once you've completed the steps above you will know what story you're telling, what information or data you need to tell it, what you want the finished project to look like, and what tool you want to use and how you want to use it. That means you are ready to go. Get started. Look back at the various chapters of this book that you found helpful as you get to work and then get out there and make something amazing.

If you get stuck, check out the help files that come with the tools. If that doesn't do it for you, search the web and see if anyone else has had the same problem and how they solved it. If all else fails, try another tool or even another approach. Remember that you know your story better than anyone else, so don't let a piece of software get you bogged down. The number of tools out there is staggering, so there has to be one that's the right fit for you and the story you want to tell. You can do it!

NOTES

1. Backspace, http://backspace.com, accessed December 24, 2014.
2. If you don't know, the full saying is "A failure to plan is planning to fail."

3

TOOLS AND APPLICATIONS

TOOLS—FREE AND LOW COST

Piktochart, http://www.piktochart.com

Piktochart is a tool for creating infographics based on templates that are easy to modify to fit your preferences for color, graphics, theme, and more. On the homepage you see a collection of beautiful and professional-looking results. From here you can tour through product features, user testimonials, case studies of how others have used the product, and Pikto Perks, which are deals and coupons for related services like search engine optimization (SEO) or a half-hour telephone marketing consultation. Pikto Perks are only available to users with Pro or paid accounts. There is also a gallery of templates and excellent graphics created by other users that are great for inspiration. The site maintains a blog with information about what's new and all kinds of tips and tricks as well as a Resources section with a search feature, video tutorials, and FAQs for how to do anything you want with Piktochart. There is even a request section to help with any specific problems you might have.

There are four pricing models for Piktochart. The Pro account is, as of this writing, $29.00 per month with no commitment beyond the current month and aimed at beginners or $290.00 for twelve months, prepaid. The Pro account gives you access to more templates, removes the watermark, increases the number of image uploads, provides privacy controls for who can view your graphic, and makes high resolution exports available. The free account is completely free but has some limitations, including a limited choice of templates, lower resolution images, and no ability to change privacy settings. The free account is a good choice for making a first try at creating a graphic. There are deeply discounted packages for nonprofit organizations including a free limited package or a $39.99 full-featured Pro account. Educational organizations can get a single-user, full-featured Pro account for $39.99 or a Classroom Pro account with thirty licenses for four months for $120.00. The discounted packages can all be customized by Piktochart to meet the needs of individual organizations.

Piktochart is an easy-to-use site that allows data importation from Excel, Google Docs, CSV files, and more. Anyone with a basic knowledge of the drawing features of Microsoft Word should be able to use it with relative ease on the first try. If you lack these skills, there are excellent tutorials and FAQs for assistance and support. Piktochart is a great choice for a beginner, with its well-featured free account option and intuitive interface.

Easel.ly, http://www.easel.ly/

Easel.ly is a free site that is template driven but allows users to start from scratch to create a truly customized infographic. It also provides an extensive gallery of infographics created by other users that can serve as inspiration. The site is ad-supported. If you want to drop the ads and gain more objects and fonts for your infographics, the quoted price of $2.00 per month is pretty good.

The editor is full featured whether you choose a pro account or not. Everything is drag and drop and can be formatted to fit your tastes. In both the free and fee accounts you can download your graphic as a PDF or high- or low-resolution JPEG file, a feature not found standard in every free version of infographic tools online. The output and functionality of the simple-to-use but powerful tool make it a good choice for a beginner or an advanced user. One caveat: There is very limited help available on the site. There is a help page on the site's blog, but the question I wanted answered had not been answered yet, so help wasn't very helpful. The site also has a page of video tutorials, but they all seem to be the same and none worked when I tested them. There is also sometimes a little message in the corner of the screen that says "Offline—Leave a message," giving me hope that someone will answer my query eventually. All of this may simply be an anomaly but I did find it a bit frustrating.

TimelineJS, http://timeline.knightlab.com/

TimelineJS is a completely free online interactive timeline creation tool developed at the Knight Lab at Northwestern University in Chicago. There is no need to register to use this timeline creation tool, nor do you need to have anything but an Internet connection and the ability to use a Google Spreadsheet (also known as a Drive Spreadsheet). The site is basically a single page so when you click Create Timeline Now you hop about halfway down the page and come to the four simple steps for making a timeline.

First, get the template[1] that works with the provided code to make your timeline. Add your information, including pictures and links, to the template spreadsheet, being very careful to leave all of the labels as they are. The timeline will not work if any changes are made to the template structure. Second, publish the spreadsheet to the web. The site includes very specific instructions for how to do this correctly. You will get a URL for the published spreadsheet that you should copy. Third, paste the URL you just copied into the Generator box and choose any additional advanced settings you like. Finally, see the code you need to publish the timeline to a website. You can also click Preview to see your timeline before you publish it. If you see anything you want to change, go back to the Google Spreadsheet and make the changes, republish to the web, and paste the new URL in the Generator box.

One of the best things about TimelineJS is that it is completely free and no login is required, although you can sign up to get updates about the tool. Also the site provides some great examples of the use of timelines and makes a slick finished product. There is a very helpful FAQ section that lays out nearly any problem you could have with the site. There is also a video tutorial to guide you through the four steps of timeline creation. You do have to have some understanding of how spreadsheets work and must be careful to leave the structure of the spreadsheet intact while deleting the dummy information that is prepopulated, but those tiny inconveniences are not too bad when you consider the ease and price of TimelineJS.

Capzles, http://www.capzles.com/

Capzles is a completely free online interactive timeline creation tool but it does require a login and nudges you toward completing a full profile, becoming a sort of social media timeline where you will want to swap timelines with your friends.

To create a Capzle all you need is the information you want to include and the ability to use a text editor that looks something like what you might find in the comments section of a blog. Once you have logged in to the site and chosen to create a new Capzle, you go to design mode. In design mode it is as simple as working your way down the left side of the screen, adding a title and description, adding tags and categories, adding content, designing the Capzle, adding a sound-track, configuring privacy, and sharing the finished product. You can do as many or as few of these steps as you choose.

Capzles provides many opportunities for very precise customization of the timeline, including the option to define colors in hexadecimal, choosing backgrounds and colors from a gallery, letting you start from a blank screen to make your creation exactly how you want it. To add music or pictures you must upload them, so be sure to keep copyright, fair use, and privacy in mind as you complete these steps. The privacy settings include Public, Friends, and Private. The sharing settings let you send your Capzle by e-mail or provide a URL that you can link a webpage to. If privacy is set to private you can still get a URL but it will take you to a Capzles page that announces that the Capzle has either been removed or set to Private.

This tool is another that has a nice gallery of projects made by others. The galleries are arranged by newest additions, top rated, and most popular. These same categories also describe what are called moments and, although they are not specifically defined, appear to be snippets of larger timelines. The galleries are worth exploring, with timelines showing the history of the U.S. stock market from 1929 to 2008 and a timeline about golf club covers—a little something for everyone.

Mindmeister, http://www.mindmeister.com/

Mindmeister is a mindmapping tool built to help users visualize ideas and concepts in a collaborative format. The tool comes in four subscription plans beginning with the free Basic plan that includes three maps and sharing and collaboration tools. Sign-up requires your name, an e-mail address, and a password. There is some push to create a profile for sharing, but it is not required. The Personal plan is intended for individuals working on personal projects who need more maps and the ability to upload their own files and images. It costs $36.00 for six months or $6.00 per month. The Pro package adds the ability to export maps into Microsoft Word or PowerPoint and provides customized themes and branding along with the ability to work in multi-user teams. The cost is $60.00 per user for six months or $10.00 per user per month. The Business package is designed for enterprise users and provides group sharing, external backups, and a custom domain for $90.00 per user for six months or $15.00 per user per month. There are also educational/nonprofit versions that are available at deep discounts, dropping the price of the Personal package to $3.00 per month for six months, the Pro package to $5.00 per month per user for six months, and the Campus plan (twenty or more users) to $1.00 per user per month for six months. All plans are available for a thirty-day free trial with no commitment to purchase.

Mindmeister provides a shared drawing board to brainstorm and plan out ideas and concepts. Maps start with a root idea and child and sub-ideas are added with a few keyboard shortcuts or the ease of drag and drop. The tool lets you link ideas from separate groupings with arrows, add labels to lines, disassociate an idea from its grouping and park it, assign tasks, add icons, comment as a collaborator, write detailed notes, and add external links. You can also begin from premade templates, change the colors and fonts on the map, upload images and videos, and turn your map into a presentation. Maps can be downloaded, printed, or shared. In addition to the online version of Mindmeister there are also Android and Apple apps for use on tablets and smartphones so you can brainstorm on the go. Mindmeister is a truly powerful tool that must be seen to be understood. Give it a try.

Creately, http://creately.com/

Creately is a tool for making diagrams and flow charts quickly and easily. It includes templates for common flow chart and diagram types but can also be used as a blank slate with simple drag-and-drop features. You can create nearly any visual representation between objects provided in the tool and those that you can upload.

The tool has many useful features. You can easily add notes to your charts and diagrams. Every shape is also a text box so it is simple to add labels to everything on the page. You can add fill to any of the objects in your diagram or flow chart. The tool also gives you opportunities to add additional objects from Creately libraries or to upload your own shapes in Visio and similar file types. The preloaded libraries include shapes for business, electrical schematics, infographics, software, and others specifically created for creating flow charts and UML (Unified Modeling Language) standards compliant diagrams. Once you have saved your work, you can download it in various formats, e-mail the image, get the code to embed it in a webpage, or share the URL with others. There is a demo version of Creately that you can use without registration, but this option prohibits saving. A personal online registration is free but has some limitations on features. An individual plan with limitations on number of collaborators is $5.00 per month or $49.00 per year. There are also online team plans for five to twenty-five users that include all features and cost between $25.00 and $75.00 per month with discounts for purchasing a full-year subscription. Creately comes in various versions including a desktop version similar to Visio and priced at $75.00 for an individual or graduated licenses for multiple users as well as plugins for Fogbugz, Confluence, and Jira. The possibilities of Creately are endless if you use a little creativity.

StatPlanet, http://www.statsilk.com/

StatPlanet is a free tool provided by StatSilk. Other products include StatPlanet Lite, StatPlanet Plus, StatTrends, and StatTrends Plus. Both StatPlanet and StatPlanet Lite are free, with the Lite version only available online and world and U.S. maps included. StatPlanet Plus is $395.00 for noncommercial users and $595.00 for commercial users. It includes all of the features of the free version but also includes additional shape files and Custom Flash that allows the user to custom design maps. StatTrends is a data visualization and graphing tool that is also available in free and paid versions and, like other StatSilk products, uses Excel spreadsheets to import data. No programming knowledge is required. StatTrends and the desktop noncommercial version of Stat-Trends Plus are available free. Other StatTrends Plus versions range from $250.00 to $395.00. The Plus version includes a more advanced feature set including more graph types, support for larger datasets, custom logos, and more export options as well as allowing the user to include seven or more indicators.

StatPlanet works in five simple steps[2] but it is very helpful to have the user guide[3] handy for beginning map makers. The program is downloaded as a ZIP file with several folders that need to be extracted for use. The user then opens the StatPlanet data editor, which is really a large and somewhat complicated Excel spreadsheet with macros that must be enabled for the mapper to work. Data is imported from a CSV or XLS file by clearing the example data and clicking import. Very large datasets take a very long time. Once all is imported, click save to put the dataset into the file data.csv. Everything in the web folder can then be copied to a website to publish or can be viewed through a Google Site or versions of Dropbox with a Public folder.

StatPlanet is very easy to use and can create some beautiful maps with interactive features and animations on a free platform.

DataFerrett, http://dataferrett.census.gov/

DataFerrett is a sophisticated data analysis tool provided by the U.S. Census Bureau to create maps, graphs, and charts of selected datasets. These sets can be sliced and manipulated according to your desires and the available data. Most of the datasets date from 2005 to the present, with some going back much further and others with variables for only the most recent years. It is a somewhat complicated tool so it is a good idea to have the user guide,[4] tips and tricks,[5] and FAQ[6] handy while you are working. DataFerrett is a Java application and runs only from Internet Explorer or Firefox. It also requires that popups are enabled.

DataFerrett allows the user to choose variables from a collection of datasets, taking as much or as little as desired. Data is then parsed and entered into a table format with drag-and-drop simplicity. Once a table has been prepared, it can be used as the data source to create maps, charts, and graphs depending upon what data is highlighted in the table. It is not a simple tool to use, but with a bit of practice anyone with a basic understanding of the way census data is provided and some ability with spreadsheets can produce nice results at no cost all in one tool.

Tableau Public, http://www.tableausoftware.com/public/

Tableau Public is a free data visualization tool that users must download to the desktop to use. It has been used by the *Wall Street Journal* Digital Edition, Freakanalytics, and UNESCO, to name just a few. The software creates workbooks that are used to create highly interactive visualizations and dashboards that can be embedded in a website or blog or shared with a URL. The tool provides a quick demo[7] that is enough to get started with a simple visualization. There is also a training page that has video tutorials and offers live introductory webinars.[8] In addition, there is an extensive FAQ,[9] a user community[10] with peer support and inspiration, and a gallery[11] of visualizations created by other users. The tool provides sample datasets for download and a listing of websites that also provide datasets in the correct formats for import.

To use Tableau Public all you need is to provide data in a spreadsheet or comma delimited file (CSV or TXT is acceptable). Your data must have a header row and shouldn't have any blank columns. Upload the data to the tool and drag and drop to create beautiful visualizations with a huge array of features for customizing the look and feel of the visualization from control of colors to addition of layers to changes in scale to show more in-depth data movement. Once you have created two or more workbooks you can combine them into a dashboard that is ready for publication. This is a great tool that is widely known and very easy to use to create visually stunning content.

Tableau Public also has a professional version, but for most users the free version offers more than enough options. When using the free version there are limits on storage space, and you must be connected to the Internet to save and manage workbooks.

Mapbox, https://www.mapbox.com/

Mapbox is a powerful tool for creating maps and data visualizations that users must download to the desktop to use. It has five plans from the free Starter to the Premium plan that is $499.00 per month and includes every possible feature Mapbox can offer. The Starter is free and provides 3,000 map views per month (a map view is fifteen tiles), 100 MB of storage space, SSL encryption for maps, and online support. The Basic plan is $5.00 per month and includes everything from Starter plus added map views, one GB storage, and Mapbox Satellite, allowing satellite imagery to be added to created maps. The Standard ($49.00 per month) and Plus ($149.00 per month) plans also increase map views and storage space.

Mapbox is an open-source tool and is designed to be used by designers, cartographers, and developers to create custom maps that can be printed, used as interactive visualizations online, used in apps like Map of the Dead—Zombie Apocalypse Survival, and used by organizations as diverse as *USA Today*, the *Washington Post*, the *Financial Times*, *National Geographic*, Pinterest, Evernote, and Bass Pro Shops. While the majority of Mapbox users are on the free version, it is being marketed to specific industries like real estate, agriculture, and transportation with needs for map creation and customization.

The tool is best used with the assistance of the available help files[12] that go from getting started to advanced topics like using Mapbox with JavaScript. There is an online editor where data is uploaded in CSV, GeoJSON, KML, or GPX formats only. The free account limits the number of attributes that can be uploaded but does provide control over the attributes used for geocoding. Once you have downloaded the software and tied your online editor to the Mapbox Studio software, you can start designing immediately by choosing a map style or uploading your own vector map that can be the MapID provided by the editor when you have saved the project. In the Studio you have control over layers, fonts, colors, styles, and more. As a beginning mapper you may want to start with the online editor and then move on to Studio when you have become more comfortable with all of the capabilities.

TOOLS—PROFESSIONAL SERVICES

Visual.ly, http://visual.ly/

Visual.ly is a website that acts as a marketplace for content creation that states its mission as

> helping you create visual content that rises above the noise. Our platform seamlessly connects designers, journalists, animators and developers with clients, featuring cloud-based collaboration tools that allow us to deliver high-quality content at unprecedented scale and speed. [13]

Visual.ly is not a do-it-yourself site, but instead acts as a sort of online matchmaker that connects organizations with stories to tell with creative professionals like designers, journalists, animators, and developers who can then collaborate in the cloud to produce professional results at prices below those that might be quoted by a brick-and-mortar design agency. The site is particularly interesting in that the work of the organization wanting graphics is really providing material, preferences, and information to the creative professionals on the team assembled by Visual.ly and paying a set, negotiated price for the finished project.

According to the website the cost for an infographic starts at $995.00, compared to an average of $4,000.00 from design firms. [14] Other services begin at higher prices. These include videos, web experiences, presentations, and micro-content. Campaigns and analytics reports have fully negotiated prices based on the complexity and work required.

Other Professionals

There are many design firms and freelance designers prepared to create professional infographics and data visualizations for a price. Most are hired by businesses that want to create a full marketing scheme with branding, design, and other services that businesses need to attract and keep customers. These services are unlikely to be the right choice for most libraries with tight budgets, but if you have the money this is a route to consider. Check out Recommended Reading for books that list some firms and freelancers as well as interviews and case studies with professionals. Don't forget to search the web for professionals in your area.

DATA SOURCES

The Internet is full of data sources that are excellent for helping you create infographics or visualize comparisons between two nearby towns to two countries anywhere in the world. Nearly all of the sources discussed below are created or maintained by a government entity and all are available free of charge online. The following descriptions are basic overviews to get you started, but you are encouraged to explore and see how this data can help you to tell the story you hope to share.

CIA World Factbook, https://www.cia.gov/library/publications/the-world-factbook/

The CIA World Factbook is a publication of the U.S. Central Intelligence Agency and is a treasure trove of information about countries, world leaders, regions, country comparisons, and historical publications. It includes a User Guide[15] that provides information on the how and what of everything on the site.

So, how would you use this font of world data in your infographics? One very useful tool is the Flags of the World,[16] providing information on the country as well as a picture and detailed description of the flag. Another great resource is the Regional and World Maps[17] that can be downloaded as PDF or JPEG files and provide political and physical maps from all over the globe. The true gem may be the Country Comparisons[18] that show countries in order from most to least for measures like land area, population growth rate, and military expenditures. Each comparison includes a definition of the measurement and the date of the information provided. This data can be downloaded in text format and can then be converted to a spreadsheet and fed into many of the infographic and visualization tools described here. One drawback to the comparisons is that the site is not set up to compare countries ad hoc, seeing how Guyana and Bolivia compare to each other, perhaps. This is only a small drawback and shouldn't deter you from using this excellent resource for gathering data you need to produce excellent graphics.

UN Data, http://data.un.org/

UN Data calls itself "[a] world of information" and it is, with thirty-four databases and sixty million records on crime, population, refugees, trade, and much more.[19] Data can be gleaned in several ways. First, there is a big blue search box on the home page where you can enter a simple search like "population of Zimbabwe" and retrieve seventy data series, including the female/male population ratio in Zimbabwe and the total population in thousands. The same search also provides table presentations that are prepopulated tables from various sources within the United Nations. All data sets and table presentations can be downloaded in XML or one of three delimited formats. The search results can also be filtered by source. The homepage also boasts a group of popular searches and links to specific databases and to the statistical or census sites of particular nations in the official language. There is a glossary of terms used in the data sets and a link to metadata for all UN Statistics Division databases. Another advanced feature is an application program interface (API) that gives web developers a way to create a real-time link on a webpage that dynamically searches UN data without the user leaving the original site.

There is an advanced search function that gives you the ability to compare two or more nations based on data sets, time periods, and search terms and creating a very specific or quite general comparison for use in your graphics. There are also premade country profiles similar to those in the CIA World Factbook. A most helpful set of tools for data visualization is available from UN data.[20] It includes geospatial tools to import into a GIS engine, several premade visualizations and graphics, a thematic mapping engine, a Firefox plugin for direct searching of the data, and the UN Statistical iGoogle Gadget for pulling country data quickly from an iGoogle page.

U.S. Census, http://census.gov/

The U.S. Constitution requires that there be an enumeration of everyone in the country every ten years for the purpose of apportioning seats in the House of Representatives. Now that data is still collected and used for apportionment, but it also provides much more. The Census Bureau not only collects data from the Decennial Census but also creates estimates of population, business, and the economy for the intervening years. There are data sets covering virtually any measure of American society that you can imagine and nearly all are available as customized downloadable information.

In addition to the data sets there are numerous tools that can be helpful in creating infographics and data visualizations. In the geographic section there are premade maps, tools for creating interactive maps, and data sets created for use with geographic information system (GIS) software to make customized maps and geographic visualizations. There are also data tools and various APIs that can make it easy to search census information from your website and quickly develop attractive graphics. The site includes galleries of sample infographics and data visualizations that you can link to from the site, embed on your site, or download as various resolutions of PDF or PNG files and related explanatory notes. The data is available in full for the 2000 and 2010 censuses and in more limited depth and breadth back to the 1940s.

Data.gov, www.data.gov

Data.gov is the U.S. government's repository for all open federal data sets and some databases from other sources including major research universities. There are over 130,000 data sets covering topics from agriculture to health to oceans and product recalls. All data sets are available for download in multiple formats. The site is also a rich source of applications for tracking air quality, locating alternative fuel outlets, and much more. The collection is meant to be a source for government transparency and a resource for innovators creating apps and other software using all of the sets made available.

Eurostat, http://ec.europa.eu/eurostat

Eurostat is similar to the information available on census.gov with a focus on the European Commission, the executive body of the European Union. The data sets include statistics for all twenty-eight EU nations from all over Europe. The Eurostat homepage features numerous popular themed data sets including population, economy, and science and technology as well as a link to the full database and the most popular tables. The site includes a treasure trove of tools and applications for manipulating the available data, including a widget that you can embed in your website to allow visualization of small portions of the Eurostat database, tools for extracting data and manipulating it, and ready-made profiles of EU nations. The data is similar to that available in the United States and might be used at a basic level as a way to compare U.S. states and European countries.

OECD iLibrary, http://www.oecd-ilibrary.org/

The OECD iLibrary is the online library of the Organisation for Economic Cooperation and Development (OECD) and also includes information from the International Energy Agency, the Nuclear Energy Agency, the OECD Development Centre, Programme for International Student Assessment, and the International Transport Forum. OECD iLibrary promises "Content for all" and "Access for all." There is a huge collection of free information available in iLibrary but there is also a subscription component that provides for organization-wide IP authentication, unlimited concurrent users, and support for usage statistics and MARC21 XML bibliographic records.[21]

The iLibrary can be searched using the big search box at the top of the homepage or using the advanced search that lets you use Boolean fields, language, content type, dates, or theme and country. A user can also browse the data by Theme, which includes everything from Agriculture to Urban, Rural, and Regional Development. As you browse you can read books and papers on specific topics within the theme, access working papers, or download data from databases and indicators compiled by OECD. When browsing by country you get a drop-down menu that segments countries by alphabetic segments. Choosing Gabon from the segment D-I provides thirty-two results including books, chapters, and statistics. These results can be sorted by date, content type, or title. Each result is also labeled by language, most often English or French. Another option is to browse by theme and country, giving statistics and other information comparing one or more themes in one or more countries. The Catalogue tab gives you access to all materials published by OECD and kept in iLibrary by type of publication, title, date, or language. The Statistics tab provides the ability to search databases, indicators (including country profiles), or book series (including the OECD Factbook) and to extract data across data sets using OECD.Stat. All searches can be limited by country.

The iLibrary contains a staggering amount of information and may be most helpful when dealing with worldwide issues like climate change and armed conflicts. It is also very useful as a reference source.

Data.gov.uk, http://data.gov.uk/

Data.gov.uk is based on a similar idea of open government data sources as data.gov in the United States. It includes central government data, much of which was already public, pulled together on a single searchable website. The site was created as a part of the Government's Transparency agenda.[22] Unlike data.gov in the United States, nongovernmental entities do not include data sets on this site.

Clicking Datasets on the Data navigation bar yields over 20,000 results. You can search within the results or use filters like theme, format, publisher, and location. Data can also be searched using a map by place name, post code, or coordinates or by drawing on the map by creating boxes with the mouse. This gives you a result list with the filtering options discussed above. Other ways to get to data include making a specific request for data not already on the site, searching for all sets published by a government entity, and using an interactive viewer to see the salaries of high-ranking public officials and the generalized salaries of other public employees.

State Demographer

All U.S. states have an office that works with the Census Bureau on the State Data Center Program. Many, but not all, have the title State Demographer. The purpose of this office is to facilitate communication for better forecasting of population growth or decline and other measures between states and the census. The information provided by your state demographer is often specialized to your area and its interests. It is often possible to call someone at the state demographer's office to get clarification or a better understanding of a bit of data you want to use but don't quite understand. While all of the information you need may be available on census.gov, the personal touch of someone who knows your state may be a big help in creating a great design.

Your Own Library's Data

Don't forget about the data you've already collected. This might be circulation statistics, budget information, cost-cutting measures you've taken, the most popular books checked out in the past year, or anything else that you capture that might be interesting to patrons or a tool for showing the importance of the library to funders, deans, trustees, and executive committees. This information, more than everything else covered above, is the meat of your story. Without it there is no story to tell. So if you are collecting it, start using it; if you don't collect these tidbits it might be time to consider starting and making it easier to tell the story you want and the story that is true.

Other Government Information Sources

Government agencies at the federal, state, and local levels collect huge amounts of data that can be of interest when creating infographics or data visualizations. State and local registrars of voting have information about elections down to the precinct level, so they are good sources to use when looking at trends in voting and demographics. Other agencies at all levels of government can also have resources that are freely available but might be hidden away on a website. The question to ask is "Who cares?" Once that is answered it's easy to determine where to look or who to call. If you need to find information about all of the brownfields[23] in your state or region, checking the state's environmental protection division site or calling to ask if the information is available can get good results. If you want to know how many doctors, or cosmetologists, or architects are in your county or city, figure out who licenses them (often the secretary of state) and see if you can find this information online. Another interesting project might be to find out who the highest and lowest paid state employees are and what sort of jobs they have by checking a website provided by most states and some other governmental entities that provides the information in an easy-to-use format with filtering and search capabilities. Sometimes being nosy and taking the time to figure out where information resides can pay off in some beautiful and impressive infographics and data visualizations on all kinds of topics with data you found for free with a bit of ingenuity.

NOTES

1. Google Spreadsheet Template, https://drive.google.com/previewtemplate?id=0AppSVxABhnltdEhzQjQ4MlpOaldjTmZLclQxQWFTOUE&mode=public, accessed December 19, 2014.

2. StatPlanet, http://www.statsilk.com/software/statplanet, accessed December 23, 2014.

3. StatPlanet User Guide, http://www.statsilk.com/files/resources/User_Guide_StatPlanet.pdf, accessed December 23, 2014.

4. User Guide, http://dataferrett.census.gov/UserResources/DataFerrett_UserGuide.pdf, accessed December 22, 2014.

5. Tips and Tricks, http://dataferrett.census.gov/UserResources/TipsTricks.html, accessed December 22, 2014.

6. FAQ, http://dataferrett.census.gov/FAQs.html, accessed December 22, 2014.

7. How it Works, http://www.tableausoftware.com/public/how-it-works, accessed December 24, 2014.

8. Training, http://www.tableausoftware.com/public/training, accessed December 24, 2014.

9. FAQ, http://www.tableausoftware.com/public/faq, accessed December 24, 2014.

10. Community, http://www.tableausoftware.com/public/community, accessed December 24, 2014.

11. Gallery, http://www.tableausoftware.com/public/gallery, accessed December 24, 2014.

12. Mapbox Guides, https://www.mapbox.com/guides/, accessed December 24, 2014.

13. About Us, http://visual.ly/about, accessed November 26, 2014.

14. How It Works, https://marketplace.visual.ly/how-it-works, accessed December 15, 2014.

15. User Guide, https://www.cia.gov/library/publications/the-world-factbook/docs/guidetowfbook.html, accessed December 15, 2014.

16. Flags of the World, https://www.cia.gov/library/publications/the-world-factbook/docs/flagsoftheworld.html, accessed December 15, 2014.

17. Regional and World Maps, https://www.cia.gov/library/publications/the-world-factbook/docs/refmaps.html, accessed December 15, 2014.

18. Guide to Country Comparisons, https://www.cia.gov/library/publications/the-world-factbook/rankorder/rankorderguide.html, accessed December 15, 2014.

19. About us, http://data.un.org/Host.aspx?Content=About, accessed December 15, 2014.

20. Visualization and tools, http://data.un.org/Host.aspx?Content=Tools, accessed December 15, 2014.

21. About OECD iLibrary, http://www.oecd-ilibrary.org/about/about, accessed December 16, 2014.

22. What's data.gov.uk all about? http://data.gov.uk/about, accessed December 16, 2014.

23. The term "brownfield site" means real property, the expansion, redevelopment, or reuse of which may be complicated by the presence or potential presence of a hazardous substance, pollutant, or contaminant. 42 U.S.C. 9601(39)(A). http://www.epa.gov/brownfields/overview/glossary.htm, accessed December 24, 2014.

4

LIBRARY EXAMPLES AND CASE STUDIES

Libraries all over are starting to use infographics and data visualizations as tools for teaching, explaining, and sharing information about the library itself, resources, and all kinds of other topics, limited only by the imaginations of library staff and patrons. A great place to see examples of beautiful library and book-related infographics and visualizations is Pinterest.[1] Pinterest is a visual bookmarking website that lets you create online bulletin boards that hold "pins" of images you find inspiring for whatever reason. Various libraries and individuals have created boards with book-related infographics from around the web. Nice pages to follow for inspiration and enjoyment include Library Infographics boards from Windsor Public Library in Windsor, Ontario, Canada; Ye Olde Fortress of Awesome; The Libraries of Stevens County, Washington; and Kishwaukee College Library in Malta, Illinois. There are even boards on data visualization by Mike Jennings and Robin Fay (georgiawebgurl) and a board of Mapping and Cartography Tools/Libraries from the Center for Collaborative Journalism at Mercer University in Macon, Georgia. A quick search on Pinterest for these libraries and individuals will bring up their boards, including their library infographics inspirations.

Libraries and other organizations are starting to see the possibilities of infographics and data visualizations as tools for teaching and sharing information about a broad range of subjects from library budgets to banned books to the history of the surrounding area. These institutions are also beginning to use other tools like those for mapping and brainstorming in new and innovative ways. These might include creating word clouds of a community meeting about library services or preparing an interactive map showing locations of branches or all libraries on campus, complete with popups showing hours and any specific information like when the library will be closed to the public for exams or staff training. These are just a few possibilities. The following are examples of how real libraries and educational institutions have made use of some of the tools discussed in this book and the experiences they have had working with this new world of visual storytelling.

The highlighted libraries and librarians had various reasons for getting started with infographics and data visualizations and used different tools ranging from completely free tools learned on the fly to having a designer with experience and professional software to make something beautiful and informative. Before you read the case studies, flip through the final products and see if you can tell the difference between the graphics created with professional or free tools.

INFOGRAPHICS IN A PUBLIC LIBRARY

Rachel Langlois is the Virtual Services Librarian for the New Hanover County Public Library[2] in Wilmington, North Carolina. The infographics she has created are featured as Peer Examples on the Library Advocacy Materials page provided as a part of the State Library of North Carolina Public Library Data project.[3]

Ms. Langlois was inspired to begin creating infographics after Library Director Harry Tuchmayer returned from a conference where infographics were showcased as a new way to display complex information and thought it might work well as a vehicle for introducing eResources, creating visually interesting annual reports, and highlighting other projects the library is working on in the community.

The first infographic came about as a part of the library's completion of the EDGE Assessment,[4] a tool developed by libraries and local governments and funded by the Bill and Melinda Gates Foundation to help public libraries make the most of technology and other resources to provide open access to information in their communities. The New Hanover Library now had lots of data and needed to find a fun and creative way to show how the library was already well aligned with New

Hanover County's goals for workforce development. The library staff knew that they had been a vital part of workforce development for years but the combination of the EDGE data and the visual power of an infographic showed stakeholders at the state and local level just *how* the library provides support beyond a dry report showing dry data and metrics.

Ms. Langlois created the infographic with Piktochart and used the EDGE data as a starting point. During the creative process she worked with Mr. Tuchmayer to create a graphic that she and the library are proud of. She says, "Once you have a good template, the rest is combining data with art. It's a lot of fun." The infographic was so successful that it was used as a part of NHCPL's presentations as a part of National Library Legislative Day[5] to show members of the North Carolina Legislature how much of an impact the library has on the citizens of New Hanover County and North Carolina.

According to Ms. Langlois, the process of creating and using infographics as tools for relaying complex information to audiences is "not a fad to make complex information easy to understand in a casual glance. The artwork translates an otherwise dull metric into a visually appealing fact or instruction." She also notes that the use of infographics has been a very positive experience for the library. "We are blessed to receive such positive support all around, but this really was the icing on the cake. Those who viewed the infographic were surprised and wanted to know more and also how we did it. They enjoyed the information and the format and got the gist of our impact on our community in a new and fresh way."

NHCPL is using infographics in many places and situations that might have had far less impact in the past. This includes recommending great books to read related to topics and events, providing complex procedures in a simple visual format, highlighting website changes, highlighting new eResources, and jazzing up the Annual Report with graphics and no more bulleted lists. The library uses infographics in all formats, including posters in branches, flyers and reports, as well as embedding them on the library website. When asked if she thinks the library will continue using this technology Ms. Langlois responded, "Heck yeah! We get a ton of use out of them as they highlight data often lost within tedious reports or they explain complex instructions in a simple and straightforward manner that is attractive and fun."

INFOGRAPHICS IN AN ACADEMIC LIBRARY

Melissa D'Agostino, Instructional Librarian at Cecil College[6] in North East, Maryland, found out about infographics during a conference presentation on using alternative assignments in the classroom and was intrigued. Recently she was put in charge of collating the data the library already collects on acquisitions, circulation, reserves, interlibrary loans (ILL), gate count, overdue notices, orientations, number of students served through orientations, and usage for each individual database subscription. She decided that instead of creating the usual report for the departmental vice president, she would instead create an infographic to make it easy to see the work of the library in a visual and engaging way.

Ms. D'Agostino tried Infogr.am first to create her infographic but found that the free version was somewhat more limited than she needed to create the graphic she wanted. She then tried Piktochart and found that it was user-friendly and that the free version had numerous options to help her make a graphic to be proud of. Once she got into Piktochart, she found the process to be very time-intensive as she tried various combinations and options to find what worked best to convey the message she intended in an attractive and professional style.

When asked about audience reaction, Ms. D'Agostino said, "Everyone loved it! Most of my coworkers are number-phobic, so they loved the pictorial representations that were much more understandable. For the same reason, it was well received by the vice president as well, who appreciated the succinctness and readability." She says she will make more infographics, especially now that she has created high expectations for the yearly statistical report. She found the creative process very rewarding and is considering other uses for infographics in the library.

The process was also professionally rewarding as the vice president and her coworkers were impressed with her decision to take a dry and boring report and turn it into an attractive presentation that anyone can understand. She thinks that this exercise probably improved perceptions of her as a librarian and as a creative person. While the library has not gained a higher profile from this use of infographics, it is likely that it will; Ms. D'Agostino plans to create all kinds of new infographics to highlight databases, provide information to faculty, and showcase student accomplishments.

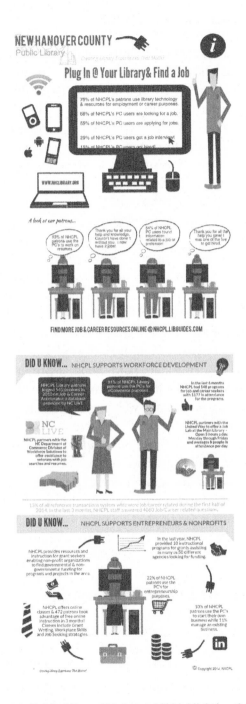

New Hanover County Public Library's infographic highlighting the library's contribution to workforce development in the county.

ANOTHER ACADEMIC EXAMPLE

Seth Allen, Online Instruction Librarian at King University[7] in Bristol, Tennessee, has put a new spin on infographics with an interactive twist. He created his infographic as an illustration for an article he recently published about using the flipped classroom model. To create the graphic, he conducted a survey of librarians who have used a flipped classroom and collected information on the model and why it might be a good pedagogical tool. He specifically chose to use the infographic style to provide the data and other information he had collected in a succinct format for sharing with his audience.

Mr. Allen chose Smore[8] as his platform for the ability to embed links and videos within the graphic. Smore calls the free graphics that it creates flyers and says it is "as easy as a marker and a piece of paper." Smore graphics are meant to be shared online, making them a nice option for libraries of all types with something to share electronically.

Mr. Allen was glad he created his infographic and plans to produce more for sharing data with fellow librarians and faculty members. He thinks the library got a boost from the infographic as it showed that the library is "savvy, knowledgeable, [and] good at presenting/curating information." He also sees this tool as a great resource for student learning. "I think we can replace static web pages on the library website with infographics—this will help digital natives better understand information literacy. I think we can create infographics about library resources/services to succinctly show the scope of what we do for our constituents. It could also replace cumbersome [P]ower [P]oints in library instruction and could be a way for students to demonstrate their learning and creativity." You can see the interactive version of Mr. Allen's infographic at https://www.smore.com/t3s5t-the-flipped-library-classroom.

INFOGRAPHICS IN A LAW FIRM LIBRARY

Thompson Coburn LLP[9] is a large law firm headquartered in St. Louis, Missouri, with additional offices in southern Illinois, Chicago, Los Angeles, and Washington, D.C. The firm has four librarians in the main office; they provide services to attorneys and staff in remote offices via e-mail, telephone, and other technologies. The library uses National

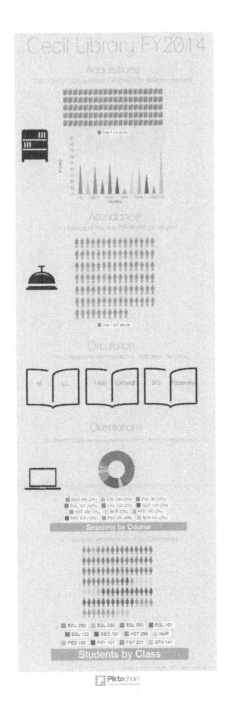

Cecil College Library Usage Statistics FY 2014.

An interactive infographic created using Smore.

Library Week (NLW) as a marketing tool to make sure that attorneys and staff throughout the firm are aware of the array of services that are provided for everyone in the firm.

Mary Kay Jung, the firm's director of Library Services, took some time to discuss her library's foray into infographics. In late 2012 or early 2013 one of the librarians at Thompson Coburn LLP gave a presentation about the rising importance of infographics as information tools at a staff meeting. After the presentation, the library staff decided that an infographic might be a great tool for reminding firm attorneys and staff about all of the services the library provides for National Library Week. While NLW was a reason for creating the graphic, its true purpose was to have attorneys and staff associate services they receive with the library and not believe that these services "just magically appear."

Another major purpose of the infographic was to highlight a large cost savings that the library realized by canceling access to LexisNexis at the end of the contract term and renegotiating the firm's Westlaw contract with more favorable terms. The library also made a number of other cancellations for a one-year savings of $491,000.

To start out, the staff chose a preliminary design, beginning with a four-column approach to highlight the major library service areas (Administration, Technical Services, Electronic Services, Legislative and Research). They chose to focus on Administrative Operations, Electronic Services, Legislative and Compliance Services, and Research Services. The library was already collecting many of the statistics they needed to create the graphic, including statistics on acquisitions, use of the Knowledge Management (KM) system, client intake, research services, ILL, training, and document retrieval. They used their existing systems to generate statistics for routing, collection maintenance, headlines, and database and wiki usage on the fly.

Once the librarians determined what they wanted the graphic to look like they were able to provide the statistics and a basic plan to the firm's Creative Services department, where one of the designers was able to put it together using InDesign. Librarians stayed in close touch with the designer throughout the process, brainstorming ways to show the information they wanted without being repetitive and being sure that the final product told the story the library wanted shared with the rest of the firm.

The final infographic was posted throughout the firm in a large poster size. Many who saw it were excited about the nearly $500,000 savings. Others were surprised by the role that the library plays in client intake. Still others asked the library staff about KM and Competitive Intelligence (CI) and how the library can help them do this sort of client development work. It was well received by the firm in general.

Ms. Jung submitted the graphic for two American Association of Law Libraries (AALL) awards in 2014, Library Publications—Print and Excellence in Marketing. The library won the Excellence in Marketing award.

When asked about the possibility of creating new infographics in the future, Ms. Jung is highly optimistic that the library will, saying, "if we can find a story we can tell in pictures, we will do it." She also noted that the exercise was great for team building among the librarians and with staff outside of the library and that it was a good experience. Other ideas the library staff is considering include the reference lifecycle or how a CI project goes from the beginning as an idea to the end as a newly engaged client, explanatory graphics for why the library chose to cancel one vendor's database and bring in another, or an illustration of how different groups use the library and its resources. Ms. Jung hopes this award-winning infographic is the start of a new chapter in library marketing at Thompson Coburn LLP.

INFOGRAPHICS IN A HEALTH-RELATED SPECIAL LIBRARY

RMC Health[10] is a nonprofit based in Lakewood, Colorado that provides training, support, and professional development for adults working with children to improve children's health and health education. RMC has a Health and Learning Resource Center that works with the rest of the organization to fulfill the mission. Courtney Drysdale, Public Services Librarian, shared an infographic she created to perk up a blog post about the library's new Read 4 Health collection. She had seen infographics in other places and thought it might be just the thing to relay some dry statistics about a fun new collection of lesson plans for teachers to use when teaching children about healthy habits. The blog post includes an interactive version of the infographic.[11]

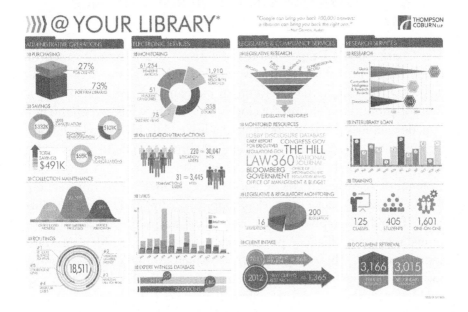

@ Your Library from Thompson Coburn LLP.

Ms. Drysdale created the infographic herself using the free version of Piktochart. She collected data about the new collection of health-themed books and lesson plans to use in the graphic. It was her first time using Piktochart, so she spent some time playing with the tool to get the look she wanted. She also used RMC Health's standard branding documents to be sure that the final product's colors and fonts looked right on the website and would be correct if used as a freestanding marketing piece.

According to Ms. Drysdale, the blog post and infographic were very well received. She plans to create additional infographics, perhaps highlighting how the library's collection is used or for promoting new items or collections as they are added. She enjoyed the creation process even though it took some time to learn to use the Piktochart tools to get the results she wanted. Ms. Drysdale is considering using infographics in the future to report annual library statistics. This might even lead to the Library and Marketing departments working together to create more attractive and engaging annual reports for this fully grant-funded non-profit organization.

DATA VISUALIZATIONS IN A NONPROFIT SCIENCE LIBRARY

The Charles Stark Draper Laboratory, Inc.[12] is a nonprofit based in Cambridge, Massachusetts. It was founded in 1933 as the MIT Instrumentation Laboratory and became an independent entity. It is now a "not-for-profit research and development laboratory focused on the design, development, and deployment of advanced technological solutions for our nation's most challenging and important problems in security, space exploration, healthcare, and energy."

Jennifer S. Swanson is a Senior Market Analyst in the Information Resources and Management department of Draper Laboratory. She created a bubble graph data visualization as a way to provide a one-page annual market intelligence plan summary to the vice president of Marketing Strategy. The summary showed which groups used the library and which groups had the most research requests. She chose to use a bubble graph because she thought it looked cool and had never had a chance to make one before.

Ms. Swanson collected data for her visualization by tracking users, the users' groups, the length of time required to complete a project (measured to the nearest half-hour), and how many requestors there were from within a group to make three axes. She entered all of this data into Microsoft Excel and used it to create her graph. To turn the data into a graph she used the Help feature in Excel 2007 to learn how to make the graphic she wanted. She did need to use some manual tweaks to enter group labels and chose to make the visualization three-dimensional because she thought it was easier to read.

The final result was just what Ms. Swanson wanted because it told the story she needed to convey in a single slide of a presentation and it was understood easily by the intended audience. She plans to create more visualizations and provide them to clients in a format that allows them to change parameters as needed. She says "I feel it makes the library look more professional and capable the more analysis we can do for [clients]." She also sees the continued use of visualizations and data analysis as something that has already improved perceptions of the library within Draper Labs and will continue to be an internal marketing tool as new employees see more and more data analysis included in

Read 4 Health

Aligning Health and Literacy

Fiction titles that support both Colorado Health Education Standards and Reading, Writing, and Communicating Standards

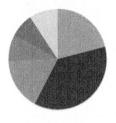

K (21%)   1st (37%)   2nd (16%)   3rd (9%)   4th (8%)
5th (9%)

Books by Grade Level

Lesson Plans to support teaching

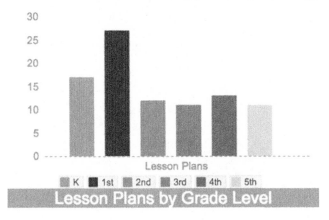

Lesson Plans

K   1st   2nd   3rd   4th   5th

Lesson Plans by Grade Level

www.read4health.org

You Are What You Read from RMC Health.

sample library research result packets during orientation. She was very happy with the process and looks forward to continuing.

TIMELINEJS FOR AN EDX COURSE

This case study is not precisely from a library but is instead from an edX[13] course. edX is a platform used by a consortium of some of the best universities and schools from around the world to provide MOOCs (Massively Open Online Classes), or classes open to anyone who chooses to take them. This example is from HarvardX: 1368.1x Saving Schools Mini-Course 1: History and Politics of U.S. Education. It is a timeline of U.S. Supreme Court cases that have had an impact on education in public schools, from desegregation to the privacy rights of students.

The timeline was created by Drew Lichtenstein, senior content developer for HarvardX.[14] He helped create the platform and content for the four-part course on Saving Schools as well as for some other Har-

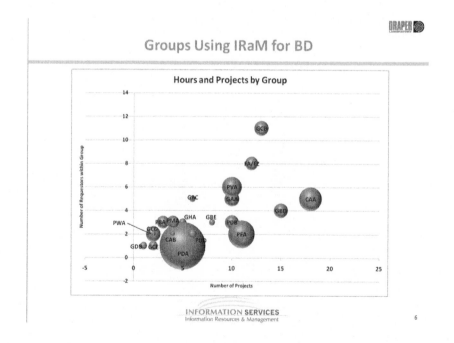

Bubble Chart of Research Requests by Groups at Draper Laboratory.

vardX courses. The timeline was used in the course as a way to pull information from several sections' worth of lectures into a coherent whole. Mr. Lichtenstein said, "We had a couple of weeks of content (Desegregation and Legalization) that were very heavy with historical details, including specific dates, people, events, and Supreme Court cases. While our professor covered all these details in the lecture, I wanted to also find a data visualization tool so students could have it all in one place (especially since the material was spread out across several videos, which was a conscious decision since we erred on the side of producing shorter videos)."

Mr. Lichtenstein chose TimelineJS as his platform because it was easy to use and was a good fit for the relatively small amount of data he needed to provide in a short time while using a free and open-source tool. To create the timeline he "watched the lectures and made notes of historical events. I then made a Google Spreadsheet of those events and dates (using Wikipedia when needed to fill in details of information). For images, I searched Wikimedia Commons and made sure all images were public domain. I then published the spreadsheet and let the TimelineJS create the timeline, though I made backups of the code in case we needed to host without their server." While there was no need for additional timelines in the Saving Schools course, Mr. Lichtenstein is likely to use TimelineJS and timelines in general in future HarvardX courses or similar projects.

FEELING INSPIRED

Only one of the case studies above used a professional designer or software. Everyone else used something already on the desktop (Microsoft Excel) or tools that are completely free or come in a free version. Each interviewee was inspired to create their graphic by a need to tell a story to a particular audience including an entire law firm, internal clients, students, and blog readers and saw some appreciable improvement in perceptions of the library or understanding by a particular person or group. Everyone had a good experience and is likely to use infographics or data visualizations in the future. Take these stories and feel inspired. No one interviewed started out as an infographic or data

HarvardX: 1368.1x Saving Schools Mini-Course 1: History and Politics of U.S. Education, Desegregation, and Legalization Timeline.

visualization expert but did start out as a person with a story to tell. Now it's time to tell yours.

NOTES

1. Pinterest, http://pinterest.com, accessed December 24, 2014.

2. New Hanover County Public Library, http://www.nhclibrary.org/, accessed January 13, 2015.

3. N.C. State Library Public Library Data Advocacy, http://plstats.nclive.org/advocacy.html, accessed January 13, 2015.

4. EDGE, http://www.libraryedge.org/, accessed January 13, 2015.

5. ALA National Library Legislative Day, http://www.ala.org/advocacy/advleg/nlld, accessed January 13, 2015.

6. Cecil College Library, http://www.cecil.edu/Student-Services/Academic-Services/Library/Pages/default.aspx, accessed January 13, 2015.

7. King University Library, http://library.king.edu/, accessed January 13, 2015.

8. Smore, https://www.smore.com/, accessed January 13, 2015.

9. Thompson Coburn LLP, http://www.thompsoncoburn.com/, accessed December 24, 2014.

10. RMC Health, http://www.rmc.org/, accessed December 24, 2014.

11. You Are What You Read: Aligning Health & Literacy, http://www.rmc.org/2013/09/08/you-are-what-you-read-aligning-health-literacy/, accessed December 24, 2014.

12. Charles Stark Draper Laboratory, Inc., http://www.draper.com/index.html, accessed December 24, 2014.

13. edX, https://www.edx.org/, accessed December 24, 2014.

14. HarvardX, https://www.edx.org/school/harvardx, accessed December 24, 2014.

5

STEP-BY-STEP LIBRARY PROJECTS FOR DATA VISUALIZATIONS AND INFOGRAPHICS

So far you have had the chance to read a bit about the tools available for creating infographics and data visualizations for your library. You've also had the chance to read about ways to plan for and execute a project. In this chapter you can walk step-by-step through projects using a variety of tools that create many different finished products. Join me as you take a look at what you can do with a little practice and planning.

PROJECT 1: USING THE TOOLS YOU ALREADY HAVE TO CREATE A SIMPLE INFOGRAPHIC[1] USING MICROSOFT WORD

One of the first projects a public library may want to tackle is a simple flow chart showing patrons what they need to do to apply for a library card. Many policy documents like library sign-up instructions are often very wordy, something to avoid when telling a story with lots of graphics and minimal text. Why not create a visual illustration of those instructions to make the process easier to understand for library patrons? In this project we will use tools that are already at our disposal to create an infographic, or information graphic, which can be used to display complex ideas or instructions such as these.

What Story Shall We Tell?

The first thing required to create an infographic is a story to tell and some data to share. In this scenario it is National Library Card Sign-Up Month and the library staff wants to tell the story of who can get a free library card and how it can be done, but not necessarily including all of the possible ways it can be done. To do this introductory exercise, look on the library's website or whatever handout is provided to library card seekers. The planned chart should make a much more concise and informative tool for patrons looking to sign up for a brand new library card.

The Power of Planning

As you should remember from the Getting Started chapter, one of the most important requirements for a successful outcome in a project like this is planning. What kind of graphic do you plan to create and what information needs to be understood from the final product? What color scheme do you plan on using? What text is required and what should be presented more visually? Are there any shapes or symbols that you consider to be must-haves and are there any you plan to avoid?

Asking the Right Questions

Your library's logo is green and blue with a touch of orangey yellow, all on a white background, so that is a very good possibility for a color scheme. The next thing to do is to list the data points needed.

- Who is eligible to get a card?
- How and where can someone get a card?
- What information does a patron need to provide?
- Do cards expire?
- Where can a patron find more information?

Nearly everyone living in the Metropolitan area, as well as teachers, students, or homeschoolers in the same area, business and property owners in the library service area who are not residents, or anyone who chooses to pay for a card is eligible to sign up.

The other answers include that a patron can get a card online and stop by any with proof of residency to pick up and activate a card or can fill out the form with proper documentation at any branch and get a card immediately, the required documentation is listed, cards need to be renewed every two years, and patrons can find more information at the library website or call a branch.

Putting the Answers into Action

To get started, open Microsoft Word to a blank document. Now is a good time to decide if you want your infographic to have a portrait or landscape orientation. Because you are creating a flowchart it is probably a good idea to start in landscape. Other options to consider now are the size you want the infographic to be. This may be determined by where you will use the infographic. Using an 8 ½ x 11 inch (letter) page layout would be good for putting this up online. If it will be used as a poster, legal (8 ½ x 14 inch) or 11 x 17 inch layouts may be better. Remember that printers in the United States will all print letter and legal sizes, but it might be a good idea to see if the color printer you have access to will print on the size of paper you want to use. Below are the ribbons you will need to use to create the infographic desired.

- **Home** provides the basic functions like font size, colors, and other tools most people use on a regular basis.
- **Insert** includes the various shapes, charts, pictures, and tables that will make up the majority of the visual elements of the infographics.
- The **Design** ribbon controls themes and colors.
- **Page Layout** is the ribbon that gives the user precise control of the page, including page size, orientation, spacing, alignment, margins, and more.

Each will be used to add structure, clarity, and visual interest to the infographic, with the ultimate goal of making an attractive and informative product.

Preparing the Canvas

First, you need to make the size and shape decisions discussed above. This infographic will be used as a poster, the largest color print the library can make is legal size, and the infographic needs to fill the page nicely so the margins will be set to narrow. These changes are made on the Page Layout ribbon.

Next choose a background color. This can be done on the Design ribbon. For this project, choose a pale blue on the Page Color menu.

Let's say the library system uses a sans serif font on the web page, so this infographic should follow suit. Sans serif fonts include Arial, Calibri, Cambria, Tahoma, and Verdana. As noted above, the other colors will be a light green and a dark blue with black type in Tahoma, a very common online font. Add a title like "Can I Get a Free Library Card?" at the top of the page just as if you were beginning to type anything in Word. Format it to Tahoma, 26 point, bold font or another large sans serif font that goes with your color scheme and house style.

Starting to Build the Graphic

Flowcharts are created with some basic shapes. On the Insert ribbon there is a Shapes menu that includes an entire set of flowcharts that will make it simple to complete this project.

Choose a shape you like and insert it. There are many options for formatting and they are all available on the formatting menu that appears when you choose a shape. Follow the same process to add more shapes, including arrows. Each flowchart shape is also a text box where the information about library card sign-up can be added. Use copy and paste to replicate anything you need more than one of on the page. Everything can be resized or reformatted to get the look you want. This is a great way to get creative with a program you can already use, even if you didn't know the power you had waiting at your fingertips.

Continue adding elements until you are happy with the results. Because the graphic is in Word it will be easy to make any needed changes later. Here is the finished product.

Can I Get a Free Atlanta Public Library Card?

Are you a Fulton County or Atlanta in DeKalb resident?

Are you a teacher in Fulton County or Atlanta in DeKalb?

Do you homeschool in Fulton County or Atlanta in DeKalb?

Are you a student in Fulton County or Atlanta in DeKalb?

Do you own property or a business in Fulton County or Atlanta in DeKalb?

YES

You can get a free card!

Come to a branch or go to http://www.afpl web.com to get started.

NO

Sorry, you are not eligible for a free card.

But don't worry, you can pay for a card.

Go to a branch or www.afplweb.com to get started.

What's Next?

Go to http://www.afplweb.com to fill out an application. You will still need to come in to a branch to activate your card.

You can also come in to any branch to apply and get your card on the spot.

You did it! Now you can check out books, movies, and music; use all kinds of databases for research; learn a language; or just enjoy the library. Congratulations and welcome!

atlanta-fulton public library system

What should I bring with me?

• Driver's license
• Student ID card
• Voter registration card
• Printed checks with current address
• Rent receipts or lease
• Social services identification
• Fulton County property tax receipts
• Current utility bill
• Parent/Guardians may use their ID to obtain cards for their children

Business owners also need to bring a letter, signed by the business owner, on company letterhead along with a business license or property tax receipt.

The finished product made in Microsoft Word.

Using Microsoft PowerPoint: Just Like Word, Maybe Better

PowerPoint has been an excellent resource for creating basic illustrations for a long time, whether the resulting slide is to be used in a slide show or as a poster or other illustration. The steps listed above for Word can easily be used in PowerPoint to make a graphic that tells the story you choose. Because PowerPoint is visually oriented by design, the graphics tools within are easier to manipulate and do not require that slides remain within rigid margins. Take a shot at designing your own PowerPoint version of the library card sign-up graphic or anything else that strikes your fancy.

PROJECT 2: CREATING A LIBRARY SERVICES INFOGRAPHIC

Introduction to Piktochart[2]

Piktochart is an online tool that provides beginners and professionals the power to create visually stunning graphics.

Create Your Account

If you have not already done so, go to www.piktochart.com and sign up for a free account by clicking on the orange Sign Up button on the top right corner of the homepage. You may also want to take a moment to check out the various links included on the homepage. Perhaps the most useful link is Resources, which includes a searchable knowledge base as well as a list of frequently asked questions that make Piktochart so easy to use for beginners and professionals alike.

WHAT SERVICE NEEDS SOME VISIBILITY?

This Piktochart project will focus on a state service providing library services for patrons who are blind or need services to assist with another print disability.

What Do We Know?

This is a project that takes some research in data sources discussed in the Tools and Applications chapter. The information used here comes from U.S. Census data and from the organization that provides services in the chosen state. According to the U.S. Census 2013 American Community Survey (ACS), there were an estimated 7,313,808 people over age seventeen living in the chosen state. Of those adults 238,844 had a vision impairment.[3] It is unclear from the available data how many adults had a print impairment beyond vision so we will focus on only those who were blind or had low vision.

Now that the who has been established, it is time to consider the what—specifically the services offered and the ways that the program can provide more services to more people who need them. The user population in FY2009, the latest data available, was 14,345, which is approximately 16.6 percent of the theoretically eligible population. These users did make excellent use of the service, checking out 423,380 items in FY2009, about 29.5 items per user.[4] These services are very similar to those offered throughout the United States. Users must establish eligibility with an application that is widely available online and requests information about the disabilities a potential user has as well as a certification of need for the service and a survey of format and genre preferences. Organizations offering services to the blind produce a catalog of materials to lend, including braille books, audio files, and specialized players, sent by U.S. mail for free, as well as services that allow registered borrowers to download electronic books and magazines from a password-protected website. The application process, password protection, and special equipment are safeguards put in place to remain on the right side of copyright.

How Does Piktochart Fit In?

Once you are ready, log in you can get started connecting the print impaired to the joys of the written and spoken word. In the past few paragraphs you have collected a good bit of data on services to the blind. We know how many people had some form of visual impairment in 2013 and how many braille and print items were circulated in FY2009 to registered users of the service. We also know what kind of materials the service circulates, what formats the materials come in, and who is eligible for this free service. We also know that the percentage of registered users is low when compared with the universe of eligible users.

Getting Started

With Piktochart you can start off with a blank slate, not unlike Microsoft Word or PowerPoint, but you don't have to. Instead you can choose from a collection of premade templates in both the professional and free versions. To get started, choose a template that you like. There are templates in four basic styles, Standard, Report, Banner, and Presentation. For the purpose of this infographic choose a standard template. For a nice start choose the Minimalist template with its pleasant colors and variety of shapes that should make an attractive first Piktochart.

To start designing, double-click the chosen template and note that it opens in an editor. With a free login some tools are not available, but nearly all of them are. Take a few minutes to click around and see all of the options available. To the left of the editor page are the major tools for changing colors, fonts, pictures, and other graphics. At the top of the editor are tools for cutting, pasting, deleting, and copying. Near the top right there are tools for downloading and sharing the finished product. Piktochart has a large save button that lets you save the in-process graphic regularly to keep your masterpiece safe. Throughout the template every element can be moved and changed as desired, meaning that if all you liked about the template was the color palette, everything else can be changed to suit your preferences.

Altering the Template

Piktochart templates are easy to change around although this project will keep nearly everything in the same locations as the original template. Leave the colors the same as well, changing a few font colors and colors of fill for changed graphics. All of this can be done using the basic tools available in the Piktochart editor. These tools are very similar to those found in Microsoft Office products and will be familiar to people who are comfortable adding text boxes and other graphics to documents. Most even have icons similar to those found in word processors and helpful menus and descriptions when the mouse hovers over them. One of the most useful tools is a set of yellow lines, like cross hairs, that are vertical and horizontal and help the user keep various elements aligned while building a graphic and moving around various pieces of the infographic puzzle.

Text Boxes and a Little More

Once the template is open in the editor choose a title and double-click on "BIG TITLE HERE" to add you own title. Clicking on a text box, or any element, shows you the text box outline with four squares in the corners to resize. There is also a small circle hovering above the box that is used to rotate design pieces. While a text box is chosen, the menu bar at the top of the screen changes to show options particular to working with text, including changes to fonts or their color or size. There are also options to change how translucent or opaque an element is and to group pieces together so they move as a unit or to arrange them so that one covers another. There is also a Preview option at the top of the editor screen. You can use this any time you like to see how the project is shaping up and what it will look like once it's complete.

A Little Bit Advanced

Another clever little menu bar pops up to the left of the canvas. This menu is a quick way to add a block, delete a block, clone it (make an exact copy), or move blocks up or down the graphic page. There is also a somewhat advanced settings menu that gives the user the ability to resize the canvas, blocks, and/or content by number of pixels. This is a useful tool when you know how large or small a space the graphic you are creating will have on a website or other media. This is good to know so that the text and graphics are a good size for easy readability. This is more than you probably want to worry about in your first Piktochart, but it is great to know it is there once you are a more confident designer.

Adding and Subtracting from the Template

Now that there is a title, the next step is to consider the content. We found out many facts about services to the blind as we planned our design, but now we need to use this tool to put it all together. I chose not to make many changes to the basic layout, but I did remove the bar chart by clicking on it to select and then deleted it. There are several ways to delete a block, including clicking Delete on the keyboard or clicking the trash can icon on the menu bar. One way that cannot be used to delete is right-clicking on a block and selecting Delete from the menu that pops up. This is an artifact of the online nature of the design site.

Replace the bar chart with a multiple-choice quiz on the number of adults with a visual impairment in 2013. Repurpose the block that says "Welcome to Piktochart" into the trivia question, resizing as needed to get everything to fit, and move the block that says "255 Units" underneath the question box and turn it into the answers by resizing the font and centering the answer choices within the block. The question might look a bit naked, so consider adding an icon. To do this, click on Graphics on the left side of the screen and select Icons. From here you can search the icon library or choose a category and browse. The icon categories start on General, so a quick browse down the list shows a question mark that might fit the bill. To add it, click on the desired icon and it will pop up in the center of the canvas ready to be moved, altered, and resized.

Moving on Up

To move a block make sure that you can see the outline with the corner squares and the rotation circle above. Hover over the icon block and a four-headed arrow will appear. Click on the arrow and the block moves anywhere on the canvas. If the block is too big, hover over a corner square until a double-headed arrow appears. Click on it and drag to make the block bigger or smaller. This resizing tool does not keep proportions equal, so be careful to make sure you like the look of a block after it has been resized. If not, just hover over the corner again and make some fine adjustments.

Charts and Graphs

You might decide you like the somewhat different take on the pie chart and keep it or choose any of the other chart options available. First add a title above the chart. The process is just like adding any other block. Click Text in the far left menu and choose from the text options shown. Click on an option you like and it appears in the center of the canvas with some dummy text. You can move, resize, change the font, or do any of the other customizations above. I moved the new title block above the existing graph block and included a title about the number of eligible users versus the number of registered users of these services. Now it's time to make the chart. This turns out to be remarkably easy. Double-click on the existing chart and a new window pops up. Here you can change the data in the spreadsheet to the statistics you found before. Put the number of registered users (much smaller) into the cell next to Axis 1 and the number of eligible users as Axis 2. Change the header in column B to Users, but this does not change the look of the finished chart. The preview here looks a bit odd because so much of the existing chart is white on a white background, but it will look correct on the existing green background. If you like, you can also give the chart a title that will appear below the graph and cannot be moved or changed separately from the chart. On the charts popup take some time to try out the look of the various options for chart types offered. Note also that you can import a spreadsheet or add a link to a Google Spreadsheet under the Dynamic Data tab. On the Settings tab you can make changes to colors, the orientation of the chart on the page, and whether the chart shows a legend or becomes static if the graphic is exported. The donut chart selected is dynamic if the infographic is used online but loses this feature when it is exported as an image file. Once you have made all of the changes you want click update chart and admire your work.

Changing Icons to Text

The next area of the template shows a subtitle and some callout boxes that have icons in them and percentages below. These numbers and pictures don't mean anything in the story of services to the blind so you may want to change them. First, change the word "SUBTITLE" to

"Who's Eligible." Next, click on the airplane icon and notice that it is not part of the callout and has been rotated to the right. To set up something like this from scratch, use the Arrange command on the top menu bar to put each block where you want it, even completely on top of other blocks. Here, the icons can all be deleted and replaced with definitions for blind, low vision, and print-impaired. The words being defined go in the text boxes that currently hold percentages and the blocks can be customized to fit below the callouts. Add three text boxes to the graphic and move each one over a callout. The default settings will place the text box on top of the callout, but you may not see anything. Except for one default text selection for this template, all of the text is white. To change this, select the text you have entered, click on Color on the upper menu bar and choose a color that you like. If you happen to know the hex value of a color you can also select that way. Add all of the definitions and then consider where to tell viewers how to find out more about the program if they qualify or know someone who does. To add this segment just add a text box, type in the text, and make any customizations you wish.

Making Blocks and Icons Match

At the bottom of the infographic you can show some of the items that the organization can provide. Two of the current icons, the book and the computer, are appropriate for our story but the plant would only work if the organization gave out gardening tips. To fix this consider the services provided. The computer is good for immediate digital downloads and the book works well for braille. The other major service provided is digital audio, so you can change the plant to a set of headphones and round out the bottom section. To do this, choose an icon from the graphics menu by searching for headphones. Choose what you like, select by clicking, and move and resize it so that it looks good with its neighbors. Unless you chose a perfectly matching set of headphones the row probably looks a bit off. To change this, select a new color. You can choose from the colors provided or select one of the other icons and click on Color and note the hex value. Enter this as the desired color for the headphones and all of the icons should match perfectly. Change the text boxes to the matching services offered and add an appropriate title to the banner to finish this section.

Wrapping It Up

You've nearly finished your first Piktochart project. There are just a few loose ends to tie up. First, be sure to give your infographic a name at the top of the editing page. Next be sure that the trivia question at the top has an answer. To do this, add a text box and choose a small font. Type the answer. The answer is currently right side up, but if you like you can use the rotate tool to turn it upside down. Click on File and Save As to keep a copy of your project in the filing cabinet. Finally, click Download to save the image, choosing image resolution and file type (JPEG and PNG in the free version). Click Publish to get the HTML code to embed in a website. The graphic will also be available to the public on piktochart.com in the free version. You can also click Share and send a PiktoCard by e-mail or share to Evernote, Pinterest, Google+, Facebook, or Twitter.

PROJECT 3: CREATING INSTRUCTIONAL INFOGRAPHICS WITH EASEL.LY

What is Easel.ly?[5]

Easel.ly is another online, template-driven infographic creator that is very popular and can be used to create infographics from thousands of free-to-use templates. The site lists its mission as "allow[ing] users to create and share visual ideas online, easel.ly." [6]

What to Teach?

In this scenario we want to teach our patrons something. Because of the passage of the National Voter Registration Act in 1993 (often called the Motor Voter Act), every state must designate "other offices" as voter registration agencies. This designation usually falls to public libraries as well as state colleges and universities. When a patron comes in to request a library card, he or she must also be offered the chance to register to vote. This next infographic will help a patron understand what is needed to register to vote and whether there are any further requirements at the voting booth.

The Piktochart Finished Product.

Getting Started

First you need to go to easel.ly and create a free account by entering an e-mail address and creating a password. That's it, no name, address, or credit card required. Next, choose a template you like from the very large selection. You can search or browse by category. I chose a checklist template, but you can pick anything that strikes your fancy or "start fresh" with a blank canvas. Next, make sure you have your plan in place, including what information is required to register to vote in your state.

A Quick Tour of the Editor

Now that you know what you want to do and have chosen a template, it's time to get going. We'll start with a quick tour of the editor and how it works. At the top of the page there is a black bar with basic commands like Home, Save, Open, Clear, Download, Share, and Logout. Below that is another bar that includes Vhemes (a variety of visual themes that can be dragged and dropped into your template, changing it completely), Objects, Backgrounds, Shapes, Text, Charts, Upload, Zoom, Grid, Undo, and Present. We will discuss each a bit more as we get to them. Below the bars is your chosen template or a big blank box if you have chosen to start from scratch. I have chosen a template that is currently in Spanish and looks like a chalkboard. It will need quite a few changes before it is ready for the intended purpose.

Altering the Template

To get started you will need to clear anything from the template that you don't want. You can do this in two ways, you can choose Clear from the Menu bar or you can remove things manually. Choosing Clear removes everything from the template and leaves you back at a clean canvas. You will get a warning to save your work before you clear. To remove items manually, note that when you move the cursor over the template it changes from an arrow to a four-pointed arrow. You can use this arrow to select any object in the template. Once you have chosen an object, a new menu bar appears that corresponds to the type of object selected. You can remove the entire object by clicking on the trash can icon or just the content of an object like a textbox, leaving the textbox for later use. Do this by double-clicking the object and an editing window will open. Make your desired changes and click anywhere outside the canvas to see the result.

Adding Your Own Material

To add new shapes, objects, pictures, text, or other material to your graphic, use the white bar just below the menu bar. Add a text box to give your graphic a title. Click text and you will see a new menu appear with three options—title, header, and body—that you can drag to where you want them on the template. Drag a title textbox to the top of the template and add your title. You will need to grab the corners of any text box to resize it to what you want. The textbox provides instructions for exactly what to do with each new box. You may want to add some body text below to give the graphic some context. The menu that opens for textboxes gives you options to change the font, size, effects, position, color, and opacity of the textbox, so you have good control over how your project looks.

Once you have finished adding your text you can start adding some pizazz with objects, shapes, charts, and uploaded images. When you click Objects on the white menu bar, a new bar opens below showing preloaded picture files you can use. They are arranged by category from Animals to Flags to Icons. Shapes works in much the same way. Pick the one you want, drag it to the template, and resize it as you like. With all of these image files you can change the opacity to make them a part of the background or bring them forward. If you want to add a chart, drag it onto your template. Double-click it and you can add titles and values for each axis of the chart onscreen without having to import any data. Add your own files when you click upload so there is no need to leave the editor if you have forgotten to upload a critical image.

Finishing Up

Now that you have your infographic all set up, it's time to save your masterpiece. Click Save on the Menu Bar and give your graphic (or visual as Easel.ly prefers) a name. Once you've done that you have several options. One is to download it in a high- or low-quality JPEG or as a PDF. You can also get a shareable link that hosts your graphic on

Easel.ly or you can get the code to embed it on your website. All that's left to do is log off and admire your job well done.

PROJECT 4: CREATING AN INTERACTIVE HISTORICAL TIMELINE TWO WAYS

Your library has decided to do a project for National Library Week that invites members of the community to come in and tell stories about life in your town since its founding in 1946 as a development built to house families and servicemen returning from World War II. Since then the town has grown into a thriving small city. The library wants to take these stories and contributed photographs and clippings and create an interactive timeline featuring everyone who has provided a memory or story. As the point person on this project, you want to look at tools to help you create this giant timeline with minimal fuss and maximum impact. To test this you decide to do a somewhat smaller project to figure out what works best for you: a few important events in 1915 from World War I to commemorate the 100th anniversary of The Great War. With that in mind, begin the project of creating an interactive timeline. One question to consider before creating something like this is where the timeline will be used. It needs to be on some sort of interactive platform—most likely a website—or the timeline will show up as a single screenshot, which is not the true goal of the exercise. You plan to put your timeline on the front page of the library website as a feature.

Introduction to TimelineJS[7]

TimelineJS is a truly free, open-source tool designed to help users build interactive timelines for use on the web. It was developed at the Knight Lab at Northwestern University in Chicago. The Knight Lab is a collaboration between Northwestern University's Medill School of Journalism, Media, Integrated Marketing Communications, and the Robert R. McCormick School of Engineering & Applied Science designed to "advanc[e] news media innovation through exploration, experimentation and education. The Lab's projects help to make information more meaningful and promote quality storytelling on the Internet."[8] The site offers beautiful examples that have been created with this simple inter-

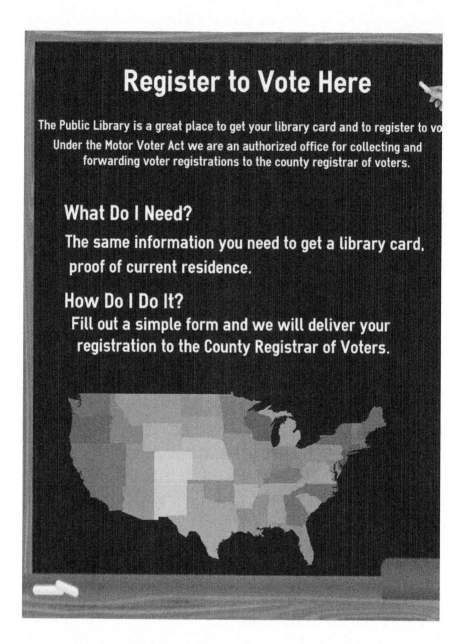

Register to Vote Here

The Public Library is a great place to get your library card and to register to vo
Under the Motor Voter Act we are an authorized office for collecting and
forwarding voter registrations to the county registrar of voters.

What Do I Need?
The same information you need to get a library card,
proof of current residence.

How Do I Do It?
Fill out a simple form and we will deliver your
registration to the County Registrar of Voters.

A voter registration infographic created in easel.ly.

face. Nearly all of the examples are from news organizations, the stated audience for the tool, including *Le Monde*, *San Antonio Express-News*, the *Denver Post*, and *Al Jazeera*.

The site requires no personal information from a user, but does require that the inputs be provided in the form of a Google Drive spreadsheet. In the help section the user is warned that TimelineJS uses the Google API to pull data from the spreadsheet, but while it is possible to start with an Excel spreadsheet: "If you want to start your work in Excel and then copy and paste your data into a Google spreadsheet, that'll work but the likelihood of errors increases."[9] If you don't currently have a Google Drive account, it is quick to set up with a Gmail or other Google account.

Getting Started

To start the process on the TimelineJS site, click on the "Make a timeline now" button or scroll down the page to the Make a Timeline section. Click the Google Spreadsheet Template button to get a copy of the template, populated with dummy information that shows what goes where. Save the template to your Google Drive with whatever title you choose. I named mine World War One. Delete everything from the spreadsheet except the column titles. Now you can enter your own data. If you hover over a column title, you will see a popup that shows whether the column is required or optional and any extra information about what kind of information can go in a particular column's cells.

Working in a Google Spreadsheet

Google spreadsheets are very much like working in Excel but some of the menus and toolbars do look different. Data entry is nearly identical to Excel. Enter your timeline facts as noted in the headings. Dates may be a single day, meaning that the Start Date and End Date are identical, or can cover a broader range of dates. Each date entry can also have a time entry if desired. Headlines can be as long or as short as you like, but note that they will be formatted by the tool, so you may see the result and want to change it. Text is anything explanatory that will go under the headline and is the first optional column.

The media columns are all optional but will make an interactive online timeline more interesting to read. If you choose to include media, note the restrictions on what can be included. The Media column includes a list of allowed links including "youtube, vimeo, soundcloud, dailymotion, instagram, twit pic, twitter status, google plus status, wikipedia, or an image." [10] If you choose to include media files, be sure to also use a media credit and a caption to give context for the viewer. You can also include a thumbnail image but this is completely optional.

Publishing the Timeline

Once all of the data is entered into the spreadsheet, publish it to the web. To do this, click on the spreadsheet's File menu and choose "Publish to the web. . . ." You will get a popup menu. Be sure that the checkbox next to "Automatically republish when changes are made" is checked. Click the Start publishing button and copy the link right above the Close button. If you go back and make changes, choose the same publish popup and click the Republish now button and copy the URL again.

Paste the copied publishing URL into step 3 on TimelineJS. Here you can change the size of your finished product and make other advanced customizations that change language, fonts, zoom, and starting point, but none of these are required to make simple timelines. In section 4 you can preview your work by clicking the Preview button. This is a good place to make sure that everything looks the way you want it. If it doesn't, go back and make changes on the spreadsheet, republish it, copy the new URL, and paste it in the publishing box. When everything is working the way it should, copy the code for embedding the timeline and add it to the website of your choice. Now sit back for a moment and hear the compliments flow before we move onto a somewhat more advanced way to create an interactive timeline.

Introduction to Capzles [11]

Capzles is a completely free online interactive timeline creation tool, but it does require a login and nudges you toward completing a full profile, becoming a sort of social media timeline where you will want to swap timelines with your friends.

Part of a timeline for the 100th anniversary of WWI.

How Does It Work?

To create a Capzle all you need is the information you want to include and the ability to use a text editor that looks something like what you might find in the comments section of a blog. Once you are logged in to the site, click Create and you have the option to create a new Capzle or edit an existing one. Clicking New Capzle puts you in Design mode. In the middle of the page you will see a white box that tells you that no content has been added and offers a useful video tutorial. After you finish the tutorial you are ready to start designing. Design mode lets you work your way down the left side of the screen to create a finished Capzle. Begin by clicking Add Title and Description. Here you can give your project a title and make changes to default fonts and colors. You can also add a description of your Capzle to help others understand what your timeline is about. Next, try adding your own tags to the Capzle and then choose any of the listed categories that it fits in.

I Just Want to Add Content

As you work down the side of the screen, you come to where you can add content. There are three ways to add one or more "moments." The simplest way to add content is by blogging it directly onto the timeline. To do this, click Blog directly onto my timeline and type your information directly into the text editor, exactly as you would on a blog. This method creates a single moment at a time. Other options include uploading content to make multiple moments or creating a stack that adds multiple files to a single moment on the timeline. In either version of uploading you can upload images, music files, Microsoft Office files, and PDFs. The upload process is just like adding attachments to a message in a webmail file or uploading in FTP. Creating a stack is just the same but requires a title, date, description, and tags from the outset. Uploaded content can be edited later to add titles, descriptions, and tags as desired.

Making It Pretty

Clicking Design Your Capzle gives you options for themes that are ready-made or for creating your own backgrounds using precise hexadecimal colors and uploading background images. You can also choose to use a two-color gradient where the colors bleed into each other or a tiled background graphic from a large collection of options. Capzles also gives you the option of adding a soundtrack by uploading one piece of music or creating a full playlist.

What's Next?

Once you have all of the design elements the way that you want them you can set your privacy options to Public, Friends, and Private. The sharing settings let you send your Capzle by e-mail or provide a URL that you can link a webpage to. If privacy is set to private you can still create a URL but it will take you to a Capzles page that announces that the Capzle has either been removed or set to Private.

Capzles creates beautiful, highly interactive timelines. For a truly multimedia project like the town history described above it is probably a better choice but you may find the stark simplicity of TimelineJS a great way to make a timeline quickly and easily.

PROJECT 5: MINDMAPPING YOUR BRAINSTORMING MEETINGS

Why Mindmap?

Mindmapping is a way to represent ideas and concepts visually.[12] You can use it to get a better handle on a new idea. You may have created mindmaps without knowing it by using a whiteboard or other medium your whole group could see to take notes during a meeting. The recorder may have drawn lines and arrows between ideas to link them visually even if they didn't come up at the same time in the meeting. Those lines are the idea behind a mindmap. It is an excellent tool for helping you think creatively while brainstorming or planning something out.

Introduction to Mindmeister

Mindmeister is a tool that helps users collaborate on mindmaps. For a library, this might be a useful way to have all branch managers participate in a web conference without leaving the branch and still have a chance to see as well as hear the ideas being discussed. You might choose to make your map public, but it will most likely stay within your organization or on your computer as a tool for planning. Mindmeister

A 1915 World War I timeline another way.

can be used by a single person or an entire group so it is a valuable tool even if no one outside of your library staff ever sees it.

How Do I Get Started?

All Mindmeister tools come with a thirty-day free trial, so you can sign up for any one you like. For this example, choose the personal subscription that is always free. Sign up with your name, an e-mail address, and a password. There is a password strength indicator that changes as you build your password. After you have signed up and activated your account, log in and you will come to an editor labeled My New Mind Map. You can change the title, also called the root idea, into something that has meaning for you. Perhaps you are tasked with planning for a new set of programs where you invite members of the community to come in to various branches and teach a class on something they know how to do like crochet, worm composting, or writing short fiction. You decide you want to call the program Each One Teach One, so that is what you will call the root idea represented by the blue blob in the center of the page. Click once and you can begin typing the new title.

I Have a Title, Now What?

To start really creating your mindmap, click on the blob again and press tab to create a child idea that you decide to call Program Ideas. Clicking on the blob and hitting tab again creates additional sister ideas that are all shown on the right of the blue blob. Click your child idea and press tab. Now you can begin typing in the ideas you've had so far for programs people might like or you already have teachers lined up for. Each idea will appear on its own line. Once you finish typing it, press enter once to lock it in and again to get a new line. You can continue adding children, grandchildren, great-grandchildren, and more from a single root idea. You can also add additional sister ideas indefinitely.

After you get through a few ideas about programs, you begin to think about who might be able teach some of these classes because you don't know how fast patrons will step up until after they see the great classes that have been set up. You click on the blob and add Possible Teachers as a sister idea. As you begin filling in names you notice that this won't mean much to other people because it doesn't link the people to the classes. To add a relationship between ideas, click on the white down arrow next to the search box and choose the rounded arrow attached to an empty circle. If you hover over it you'll see that it is called Add a relationship between ideas and that the shortcut is [Alt+C]. Click on the icon and then connect someone from the possible teachers list to a class topic. An arrow that looks very much like the icon appears and now the map makes a bit more sense for someone who isn't you.

Everything in Mindmeister is drag and drop. Perhaps you've decided that the worm composting notion wasn't the best idea right now but you want to keep it on the map as an idea that can be considered later. In many meetings this is called putting something in the parking lot. Here you want to park the worms in the corner. To do this, click and drag the worm composting idea away from the parent topic and kind of yank the mouse to unmoor it from related ideas and create a floating topic.

What Else Can I Do?

There is so much available in Mindmeister that it really needs to be used to truly understand it. So far you have seen the basics of how and why you might want to mindmap. Other options available in the tool let you add labels to lines, assign tasks, add icons, comment as a collaborator, write detailed notes, and add external links. You can also begin from premade templates, change the colors and fonts on the map, upload images and videos, and turn your map into a presentation. Mindmeister is a truly powerful tool that must be seen to be understood. Give it a try.

PROJECT 6: CREATING LIBRARY WEBSITE FLOWCHARTS AND DIAGRAMS USING CREATELY

There are many great reasons to create diagrams and flowcharts in a library setting. Perhaps you are planning a library move and need to create a diagram of the new shelving versus the old so you can see how things will fit. Maybe you have volunteers or students who work at the circulation desk for short periods of time and you want them to have an

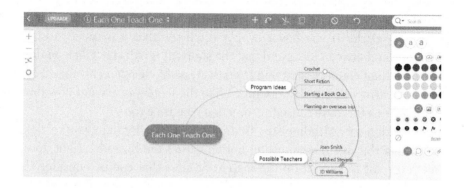

The beginnings of a mindmap.

easy-to-use reference to know what to do if they need to help someone with a reserve item or an inter-library loan. This is a job for Creately.

Introduction to Creately[13]

Creately is a tool specifically for creating diagrams and flow charts with drag-and-drop simplicity. The tool can be used in Demo mode without signing in, although this mode does not allow saving. The free Public plan online allows for saving and the rest of collaboration and five diagrams. There are many other plans, including a desktop version and educational/nonprofit pricing.

Diagramming a New Library Website

It's time for your library to give its website a facelift and it's your job to come up with an initial plan. To get started you want to sketch out a sitemap as a roadmap for the project. Making this kind of diagram is simple in Creatly. To get started, click the New icon on the toolbar. You should get a popup inquiring about what you want to draw. You can type into the search box or skip this step and start from a blank canvas. Try typing website and see that you get no diagram types in the dropdown box. Now just click in the search box and then scroll down to Sitemap, which looks like just what you had in mind. You can choose a type and then choose between starting from a blank diagram and picking a template as your canvas. Choose any of the templates that you like. Once you have a template selected, you can give it a name and description and get started.

Getting the Mechanics Down

The background of the template is set up like graph paper, but there is no automatic ruler available so you will need to determine a scale. Decide which of the pages in the diagram work for you and which you might want to delete. Once you have this starting point, you can begin the diagram by dragging and dropping shapes from the shapes library. The new shape will expand and a toolbar will appear above it. This toolbar gives you options including editing text, connecting the shape to something else, ordering shapes, linking to a URL, or creating a one-click shape that is basically the clone of what you just dragged in. Use the textbox feature of each shape to label it as the page you expect it to be.

You can add identical shapes easily by using the one-click shape feature. The two shapes come automatically connected by a line, but that can be removed by selecting the line and clicking Delete. You can select multiple shapes by holding down Ctrl and clicking each of the shapes you want to keep together. Click Copy and Paste on the toolbar and create identical pages, continuing to label as you go. Note that as you add text you should press Tab to commit to a text change instead of clicking Enter, which only adds a hard return.

Top Down

Starting with the Homepage, you want to create a diagram that looks something like an upside-down tree. The Homepage links with lines that run down and across to the pages that will appear on the side or top navigation bar of the redesigned website. Some may be exactly like your current site and some will be new. You know that the important things to have highly visible are How Do I?, My Library Account, Catalog, Electronic Resources, Find a Branch, About Us, and Contact Us. You may need to add additional pages to the template you have chosen. This is a good place to use the cloning feature discussed above. You can link these new pages to the old ones with lines by clicking Line on the toolbar at the top of the canvas. You can use a series of straight lines or choose a new line type that produces a sharp angle. Getting lines to go where you want takes a little practice, so be patient as you start drawing. Lines can be adjusted for color and thickness using the toolbar above a selected line.

Now you need to decide what should go under each major link. To do this just drag and drop pages from the shapes menu. You have several options, including a New Page, Page Cluster, and Future Page. You can see in the example that all three types are used. New Page is good for single pages that already exist, like the Catalog. A page cluster is good for places where you know there will be a number of options that will need to go under the main page but save space on the sitemap diagram. Future pages are placeholders for pages that haven't been created yet. In this example, those are the pages for the branches that branch managers will be in charge of providing content for and updating as needed. Continue adding pages and lines until you have a diagram that looks like it includes what needs to be on the newly redesigned website.

There are also a few useful icons you can use. In the example there is a lock icon on My Library Account and Research Databases—Offsite Access. This shows that a user needs a username and password to gain access. There are also green arrows on the Overdrive and Zinio pages, showing that these link to external sites, even though a library user may not be aware that they have left the library's webpage.

Other Nice Features

Creately has many features. For the diagram example above, you can add notes to the diagram that will stay with it. You can add fill to any of the objects in your diagram or flow chart. The tool also gives you opportunities to add additional objects from Creately libraries or to upload your own shapes in Visio and similar file types. The preloaded libraries include shapes for business, electrical schematics, infographics, software, and others specifically created for creating flow charts and UML (Unified Modeling Language) standards compliant diagrams. Once you have saved your work, you can download it in various formats, e-mail the image, get the code to embed it in a webpage, or share the URL with others. The possibilities of Creately are endless if you use a little creativity.

PROJECT 7: CREATING INTERACTIVE MAPS WITH IMPORTED DATA

Maps are one of the most classic forms of infographic, providing information about land masses and bodies of water along with other physical features or manmade features like national borders, city limits, and streets. In the age of interactivity, maps can also become data visualization vehicles showing population movements, changing borders, or information about a place, like education, poverty, or literacy levels. In your library you might be asked to prepare an online display of areas of conflict throughout the world or a map that shows patrons or students the various ethnicities that make up your city, county, or country. For this example you will use StatPlanet to create a world map of measles immunization rates with data from the World Bank and a map of aggregate public library circulation in 2012 in the United States using Census data and DataFerrett.

Introduction to StatPlanet[14]

StatPlanet is a free tool provided by StatSilk. Both StatPlanet and Stat-Planet Lite are free, with the Lite version only available online and with world and U.S. maps included. StatPlanet works in a five simple steps

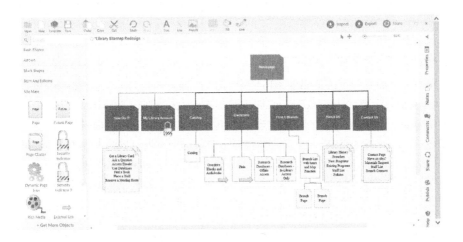

The new library webpage redesign in progress.

but it is very helpful to have the user guide[15] handy for beginning map makers. The program is downloaded as a ZIP file with several folders that need to be extracted for use. For this example, you are the librarian at a hospital and you have been asked to help create a campaign showing the importance of vaccination. You decide to create a world map that will show what recent trends in immunization for measles have been around the world. It will be used online so you would like to make it interactive and animated.

Who Has the Data?

As you get started, you need to find data on the measles vaccination rate around the world. You consider who might collect this information and decide to see what the United Nations has available. You go to the UN Data site[16] and find data from the World Bank on the immunization rate for children ages twelve to twenty-three months. Click View data and select the filters you want to use. In this case you will not include any filters on country but will filter by year, choosing 2012 and 2013. Choosing more years than that makes the import process very long and prone to errors, so two years are sufficient for the example. Be sure to check that you have no extraneous fields that will cause problems with the data structure. Refer to the user guide if you are unsure about how the data structure should be formatted. Click download and choose the format you prefer. Selecting comma will give you a CSV file, one of the most commonly used download formats.

Starting Up StatPlanet

To get started, download[17] the ZIP file containing the StatPlanet files and extract them on your computer. Depending upon your extraction program, this may happen automatically when you click on the file or you may need to do the extraction manually. Because you are creating a world map you should open the World_map folder and double-click on StatPlanet data editor to open it. The data editor is really just a large multi-page Excel workbook with macros that must be enabled for the mapper to work. If you work in a setting that does not allow users to enable macros for security reasons, you may need to use another computer for this project. Once macros are enabled, the buttons on the top of the first page will work. Click Clear data to remove the example data from the spreadsheet and click Import data to add your dataset. Data is imported from a CSV or XLS file. Very large datasets take a very long time and slow the computer down considerably, so it may be best to do your import at a slow time in your workday or after hours. Once all of the data is imported, click save to put the dataset into the file data.csv. If you choose, you can use some of the advanced options for data import, file structure, and customization that are discussed in depth in the User Guide. For now saving the import as is should suffice.

Let Me See

To see your map you need to publish it. This can be done by copying all of the contents of the StatPlanet web folder to your website server to publishing it online. If you would like to see it before it goes out to the world, you have several options. Click StatPlanet.exe and run it and your map should be viewable offline. You can also open StatPlanet.html to view your results in a browser. The author had trouble getting either of these options to work, but there are workarounds. If you have a free Dropbox account that was created before October 4, 2012, you can use the Public folder to publish your map.[18] You can still use a free option with Google Sites.[19] If you have a Google account, go to sites.google.com and sign in. If you do not have an account you can sign up for one for free. You may have already done this to use TimelineJS, described above. Once you are signed in, click on the tools icon that looks like a gear and click Manage Site and then click attachments. Click upload and copy over all files from the web folder.

Introduction to DataFerrett[20]

DataFerrett is a sophisticated data analysis tool provided by the U.S. Census Bureau to create maps, graphs, and charts of selected datasets. These sets can be sliced and manipulated according to your desires and the available data. Most of the datasets date from 2005 to the present, with some going back much further and others with variables for only the most recent years. It is a somewhat complicated tool, so it is a good idea to have the Users Guide,[21] tips and tricks,[22] and FAQ[23] handy while you are working. DataFerrett is a Java application and runs only

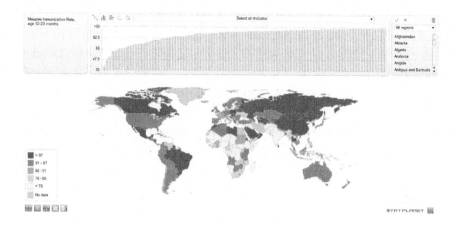

This is how StatPlanet shows the imported data via a Google Site.

from Internet Explorer or Firefox. It also requires that popups are enabled. Once you have the setup complete, click Launch DataFerrett and you are ready to start ferreting out data for yourself.

Using the Tool

The first thing you will see on launch is a popup box asking for an e-mail address. There is no requirement to provide an e-mail address, but it is only used to e-mail larger data files if required and you will be asked each time you open the application. You cannot use the application without an e-mail address. Like many of the tools you have seen so far, this one is based on tabs and works across the top of the screen. The first page you see is the Introduction; it includes tutorials, examples, a link to the Users Guide, and information about the available datasets. Take some time to explore this page before you get started. When you are ready, click Step 1: Select Dataset & Variable.

Pulling the Data

The first screen you see is somewhat intimidating, with a long list of datasets, a search bar at the top, and a big empty box. As you take a quick tour around you see that you can choose specific data types: Microdata, Aggregate, Longitudinal, and Time Series. All are currently checked and you can leave them that way or can change them if your data needs changing. In the list of datasets you will see Public Libraries Survey. Click on the plus and note that there are six datasets covering 2007 to 2012. Click the plus next to 2012 and note that there are three topics: Administrative Entity, Public Libraries Survey, and State Summary Characteristics. Clicking on any one gives you the option to see a description or view variables. The description goes into great detail about the reason for the dataset, how data is collected, methodologies, and any caveats that should be considered when using the data. Choose View Variables under 2012 for the subset Administrative Entity. The big empty box now shows two variable types: Selectable Geographies and Administrative Entity variables. Select all topics by checking the boxes or clicking the button above and then press the newly available Search Variables button.

Now you can start picking the variables that you want to show in your map. You can do this by holding down Ctrl and clicking on the required variables. You must include a Selectable Geographies variable or the program will be unable to create a map. Choose one of the Selectable Geographies and Total Circulation and any other variables you like. When you are finished, click Browse/Select above the variable list. You should get a message that you have selected geographic and nongeographic variables and should click okay. If you don't get this message go back to the variable list and check what you have chosen.

A new window appears called the Ferrett Geography Codebook with three boxes. The one farthest to the left shows the geography options available to you, the middle shows hierarchies, and the right shows what you have chosen. You can double-click or click and drag a data type to the selected variable box on the right. Dragging over County shows that the hierarchy is FIPS State Codes >> FIPS County Codes. A list of state names will appear in the left-hand box. Choose one or more states or click select all and drag to the right-hand box. Click next level and a list of county names appears. Follow the same procedure as you did with the states, making sure that the top of the right-hand box says that a reasonable number of variables were added. If you have chosen all states and all counties you should have over 3,000 selected; if you only have fifty-two, try dragging again. When you are satisfied, click finished. You may need to resize the popup window to see the Finish button. Another window should have opened underneath the Codebook. This is where the rest of your variables are. If everything looks right, click Select All Variables and then click okay. You will get a message that tells you how many variables were added to your DataBasket.

Setting the Table

Before you can make a chart or map you need to set up a table in Step 2: DataBasket/Download/Make a Table. Click the Step 2 button and a new window will open that show the variables you have selected and gives you another opportunity to go back and make any changes necessary. You can download your data here or click the Make a Table button. Once you click, you will get a new popup message with instructions for making a table. Click okay and continue.

The next screen looks like a typical spreadsheet with the rows labeled R1, R2, R3 . . . and columns labeled C1, C2, C3. . . . Now you can simply drag and drop variables into the rows and columns, being sure to keep the cell at the intersection or R1 and C1 empty. Start by dragging GEOG-102 County to C1/R2 and all counties selected earlier will populate in that column with the column directly to the right populated with question marks. Drag any other variables you like to R1/C2 and so

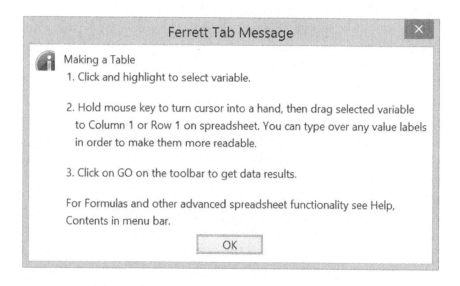

Instructional Popup from DataFerrett.

on until you have all of your labels set. You will see that all you have for data are question marks. To solve this problem click the neon green GO Get Data button the tool bar. Your table will soon be populated with the data for each variable you chose.

Let's Make It a Map

To make a map you need to select all of the data for one or more variables. Because you chose counties, this part may take a little while. Once you've selected the desired data, click the map outline on the toolbar and a new window with a map will appear before your eyes. It may not look perfect yet, but you can change its appearance in several ways. You can change the size manually by changing the number of pixels for height and width, much like you would for monitor resolution. Your map defaults to displaying data in intervals. You can change this to make the data display in quantiles instead of equal intervals under Map Type on the View menu. You can also define custom intervals and value ranges for the data. You can also add state, county, and water borders under layers. When you are happy with the map, save it as a JPEG or print it from the File menu.

Maps aren't your only option. You can also choose to create charts and graphs from bar charts and scatter plots to pie charts and pyramid graphs. All of the graphs can be manipulated for size, color, and label and legend schemes, similar to the editing options for maps. Everything that you are able to create with DataFerrett is dependent on the data you select in the table you created. If you are not able to create the desired visualization from the data provided, the associated icon is grayed out on the tool bar. Just change what you have selected and you should be able to create anything in the DataFerrett repertoire.

PROJECT 8: CREATING COMPLEX DATA VISUALIZATIONS

Complex visualizations involve multiple variables and often are made to be interactive and dynamic. These visualizations can take many forms, including maps, three-dimensional graphs, and charts with sliding time scales or other features. In these projects you will work with free tools

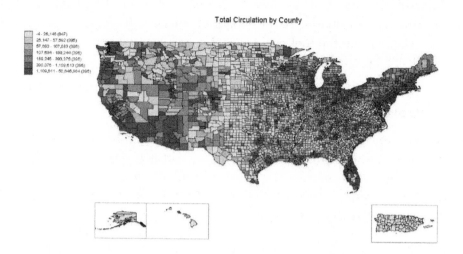

Total Circulation by County

A DataFerrett map showing library circulation by county.

that require some additional skills including preparing data for import and manipulating data points in a less structured environment than in previously discussed tools.

Introduction to Tableau Public

Tableau Public is a free data visualization tool that users must download to the desktop to use. It has been used by the *Wall Street Journal* Digital Edition, Freakanalytics, and UNESCO, to name just a few. The software creates workbooks that are used to create highly interactive visualizations and dashboards that can be embedded in a website or blog or shared with a URL. The tool provides a quick demo[24] that is enough to get started with a simple visualization. There is also a training page that has video tutorials and offers live introductory webinars.[25] In addition there is an extensive FAQ,[26] a user community[27] with peer support and inspiration, and a gallery[28] of visualizations created by other users. In the example for Tableau Public you want to show the brownfields in your state, how many acres are currently in various phases of cleanup, and the status of the waste causing the sites to be classified as brownfields. You go to your state government's environmental protection agency and find the division in charge of brownfields and happily discover that there is a newly updated spreadsheet listing all brownfields currently monitored by the state.[29] Download the spreadsheet and you are ready to get started.

Getting Started

You will begin at the Tableau Public homepage. The fastest way to learn to use the software is to watch the How It Works tutorial discussed above. If you want some more in-depth training, look at the FAQ and check out the training options offered, including the free webinars that are scheduled regularly. Now is also a good time to sign up for an account. This requires a valid e-mail address, a screen name, and a password. An account is required for saving your work in the software. You should also go ahead and download the software executable and install it as instructed. Even though the manipulations are made in software, you must have an Internet connection to view or save your visualizations.

Once you have everything set up, open the software package and take a few moments to look around at the opening page. From here you can get started by importing data and can also view the quick tutorial again—see the "Viz of the Day"—and find templates and sample data-sets to use for practice. When you are ready to get started, click Open Data to begin. Datasets can be imported as XLS or TXT file types. If you have a newer version of Excel, the XLSX file type will also work and comma and other delimited files will work as text files. Choose the file you want to import. It will take a moment or two for the file to upload. Once it has finished, drag the sheet or sheets that the software has determined are in your spreadsheet to the data area at the top of your worksheet. Just as in spreadsheets, workbooks contain worksheets, so your full project will be contained in a workbook, with individual elements saved as worksheets.

Starting the Manipulation

Start your first worksheet by dragging data from the indicator (geo-graphic, text, etc.) and numeric sections created from the imported spreadsheet into the rows and columns shown at the top of the screen. Your sheet will begin to populate with representations of the kind of data you have chosen. On the right side of the screen you will see a collection of visualization types available. Only the ones that can be made with the data you have chosen will be available, with others grayed out. As you change and rearrange your data, you will see the possible visualizations change before your eyes. From the available data types, include latitude in rows and longitude in columns and then choose the map icon at the top left of the visualization types. Your map will appear in place of the chart in the center of the screen. You can now begin designing the map by altering its appearance. That includes changing the look of the map background, changing the washout level, zooming in or out, adding state and county border lines, and more. You can also change the look of the data points on the map by changing shapes, sizes, and colors. Once you have the map the way you want it to look, save it. Saving the sheet does not give the map a title. To do that click on Show Title in the Worksheet menu. A Title bar will appear below the bars for rows and columns. Click on the bar and choose a descriptive title to make your work more understandable and useful to the viewer. If you are logged in to Tableau Public you will be prompted to choose a file name and then save. If you have not yet logged in you will need to do so and then follow the instructions to save. Once you have saved a worksheet, you will go directly to a screen that provides you with options to share or publish your map. You could stop here and publish to your webpage or blog but Tableau Public offers more options to create an even more compelling story with the addition of charts and graphs, so let's keep going.

A Few Small Additions

To create additional visualizations in the same workbook, click on a new sheet at the bottom of the workbook and follow the steps above. Changing the order and location of the indicators in the bars at the top of the sheet will alter the visualization options. This time drag Cleanup Plan and Cleanup Complete to the columns bar acreage as a sum to the rows bar. Now select a different chart style like the area chart (discrete). Remember that you can only choose visualization types that are possible with the data you have provided. The customization options on the left side of the screen will change and you can set colors and other features of the graph as you want them. Title and save this sheet as before.

You decide you would like one more chart to give your audience another way to view the data and understand the story you want to tell them about brownfields and the environment in your state. To show the same data you have in the chart above, click on the button to clone your recent worksheet. You will see exactly the same worksheet with the same data in the same places. Change the visualization type to a packed bubbles chart and now you have the same data that tells your story three different ways. The customization options on the left side of the screen will change and you can set colors and other features of the graph as you want them. Title and save this sheet as before.

Three Pretty Pictures

The three pretty pictures you have just created, a map, an area chart (discrete), and a packed bubble chart, are all great on their own and each tells a part of the story. Put together, they will tell an even more powerful story. This calls for creating a dashboard. To open a dashboard, click on the Dashboard menu and select New Dashboard. A new sheet will open called Dashboard 1. To use the dashboard, all you need to do is click and drag your map and two charts over. Tableau Public alters the color scheme of your charts so that both can use the same color legend. Now you have four elements on the dashboard, your map, the area chart (discrete), the packed bubble chart, and a legend showing the colors used and what they mean. Your dashboard has lots of possibilities for changing appearance. The left side of the screen now includes options for changing the layout of the dashboard and changing the shapes and sizes of the data elements for a truly custom look. Take some time to move objects and change formats with the simple drag-and-drop functionality. Be sure to add a title so that the user knows what they are looking at. Save your dashboard in the same way you have saved your worksheets before and you now have a beautiful story from what were once just three pretty pictures.

Sharing Your Work

You didn't do all of this visualizing just to hide it under the bushel of your desktop. This was meant to be shared. Once you have saved the dashboard you will get the option to Preview or Share it. Preview gives you a chance to see what your work will look like online. Take a little time to play with it, clicking all over and seeing what appears in the popup boxes when you hover over a data point on the map or either graph. If you see something that you want to change, you can always go back to the workbook and make any alterations you like.

Click on share and now you can copy the HTML text to embed into your webpage or blog or choose the share options to e-mail or otherwise send the URL to yourself or someone else. While your dashboard would make a beautiful poster or other static object, it is meant to be experienced online, so use it somewhere that allows manipulation if at all possible.

As you have seen in this section, Tableau Public is a very powerful tool that is free for anyone to use. It provides sophisticated tools that create professional results in attractive packages for use online or in other interactive environments. If you work in an environment that has locked-down computers, be sure to request permission to download this free and widely used tool to provide you with the opportunity to do visualization work that is beautiful and educational.

Introduction to Mapbox

Mapbox is a powerful tool for creating maps and data visualizations that users must download to the desktop to use. It can be used in a completely free version with some limitations, but also has fee versions that provide additional storage space as well as options for uploading more data with more variables and indicators.

Mapbox is an open-source tool and is designed to be used by designers, cartographers, and developers to create custom maps that can be printed, used as interactive visualizations online, used in apps like Map of the Dead—Zombie Apocalypse Survival, and used by organizations as diverse as *USA Today*, the *Washington Post*, the *Financial Times*, *National Geographic*, Pinterest, Evernote, and Bass Pro Shops. While the majority of Mapbox users are on the free version, it is being marketed to specific industries like real estate, agriculture, and transportation with needs for map creation and customization. For Mapbox you decide to do a map showing all libraries on campus.

The tool is best used with the assistance of the available help files[30] that go from getting started to advanced topics like using Mapbox with

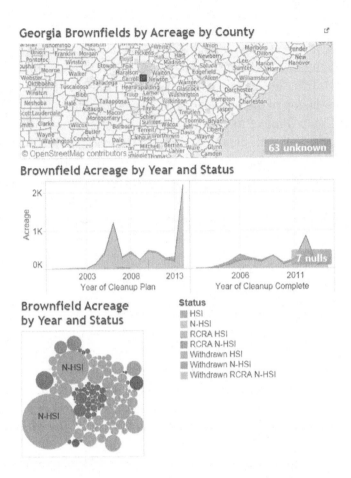

Here is your dashboard once it all comes together.

JavaScript. There is an online editor where data is uploaded in CSV, GeoJSON, KML, or GPX formats only. The free account does provide control over the attributes used for geocoding. You can use the tool's online editor and the downloadable Mapbox Studio together to create stunning and useful maps of all kinds. While Mapbox claims to create visualizations, the results are all really maps with varying levels of inter-activity and movement over time and space.

Getting Started

To get going, start at the Mapbox homepage and create a login with your name, a screen name, e-mail address, and password. Now is also a good time to download the software for Mapbox Studio, although you won't use it for a little while. Once you have done all of that, click on Projects at the top of the screen to go to the online editor.

Click Create Project to get started in the editor. A new project will show a world map with blue water and brown land. Here is where you can make the magic happen. Click style to see the various customizations for color palettes, map features like roads, borders, and water features, and the language you want you map to appear in. You also have the option to change the base layer of the map from streets, to terrain, or to satellite images. For this project you choose streets.

Where Are You Going?

Clicking data gives you options to draw on the map or select data to import. You don't currently have any data to import in the required formats of GeoJSON, CSV, KML, or GPX, so you choose to draw. If you were going to use an imported file, be aware that there is a limit to how many indicators you are able to import when using the free version, so drawing may always be a good choice unless you decide that you will use Mapbox regularly and want to pay for one of the various subscription models.

You are currently looking at a map of the world, but your campus isn't quite that big. To shrink the map down to size, you can click the purple hand icon and use it to pan to the area of the map you want. You can also use the plus and minus signs at the bottom left of the screen to zoom in and out. You will see the latitude and longitude change as you zoom. You want a very specific location, so you click on the magnifying glass icon and a search box appears. Enter the address of the first library you want to mark. Suggestions will appear as you type. Once the address you want appears, click enter and the location will appear on the map. Double-click on the address label and add a title and description. Tabs along the bottom give you options to change the place marker's style, color, or symbol as well as get exact latitude and longitude. Save your work by clicking save. You may need to reenter your password to complete the save operation. Now click on the place marker and see that there is now a popup with the library's name and any description you added.

Continue adding libraries until you have them all. Not all addresses register in the Mapbox search feature. If this is true for you, click Data and then select Marker. Now you will see that the hand has become a plus sign. Click where your location should be and a location marker will appear. This marker can be manipulated in the same way as all of the other markers you have placed. You may want to make changes to the project, like color coding the various kinds of libraries or choosing different symbols from the many available. In this example, one library is housed inside the main library. Mapbox does not allow you to have two markers at the same location, but you can add information in the description field explaining this.

Saving and Sharing

Once you feel that you have everything where you want it, save your work again and click Project. To name your project, click the Settings tab below the Project area and add a title and any description you want for your map. From Project you can also access the Info tab. Here you can download your work as KML or GeoJSON files, copy the MapID for use with JavaScript, iOS, and web services app development, copy the URL to share your map, or copy the code to embed the map in a webpage. Once you have done what you need to do here, save your work once more.

Now you have two options. You can save your map as is and share the URL or embed it on a webpage. If you take this approach, congratulations on creating a great map.

Going Advanced

You can also pull you map into Mapbox Studio to add advanced customization features. To use Mapbox Studio you may first need to tie the online editor to the software piece. This can be done easily by following the screen instructions and logging into your account if required. To add your map to the software, you may need to return to the online editor and copy the MapID to the clipboard under Projects >> Info. On the Studio start page, scroll to the bottom and paste the MapID and click Create. Your map appears near the center of the screen, with a stylesheet window on the right and a toolbar above and to the left of the map. You can use this tool to change fonts, embed new features, make fine adjustments to colors, add map layers, or use HTML and XML coding to change the default stylesheet.

For most library users, this step is unnecessary for creating an attractive map and is likely to be frustrating even with the guides and FAQ[31] provided. Please feel free to give it a try and see what great things you can create with this free and very advanced tool. There is also online help that can assist you in using the software. Mapbox Studio is really built for app developers and cartographers who have a need for very powerful mapping software.

SUMMING IT UP

Now that you've had a chance to see all of these tools and techniques, it's your chance to figure out how you want to use them to tell your library's story. Remember that these examples are created using just a small subset of the huge universe of visualizations. If none of these tools strikes your fancy, take some time to search for more. There are more and more tools to create infographics and data visualizations popping

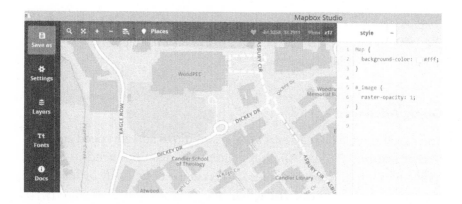

Here is what you will see if you start work on an advanced map in the Mapbox Studio software.

up online all of the time, each one adding more features, customizations, and templates to create visualizations that are more sophisticated and attractive than ever. These new tools will most likely also be more intuitive and easy to use with improved drag-and-drop capabilities and other feature additions. Feel comfortable choosing the tools and techniques that work best for you and for your institution. Remember that just because you can create something beautiful, that doesn't make it meaningful for your audience or successfully tell the story you have in mind. Use the right tool for the job at hand and your storytelling will be successful and meaningful. Good luck and have fun!

NOTES

1. The Microsoft Word and PowerPoint projects were created using Word and PowerPoint 2013 on a PC running Windows 8. Although the results should be very similar for Office 2010 and 2007, this is not guaranteed, so please check the program's help file or a manual if something looks very different or a button or menu is not available to you.

2. Piktochart, www.piktochart.com, accessed December 19, 2014.

3. Source: American Fact Finder, U.S. Census 2013 1-Year Estimates, American Community Survey, http://factfinder2.census.gov/rest/ dnldController/deliver?_ts=430944738692.

4. Source: State of GLASS Report, 2009, http://www.georgialibraries.org/ glass/state_of_glass0909.pdf.

5. Easel.ly, http://www.easel.ly/, accessed December 19, 2014.

6. About Us, http://www.easel.ly/blog/about-us/, accessed December 20, 2014.

7. Knight Lab, http://timeline.knightlab.com/, accessed December 19, 2014.

8. Knight Lab, http://knightlab.northwestern.edu/, accessed December 19, 2014.

9. Knight Lab, http://timeline.knightlab.com/#show-faq-can-i-use-excel, accessed December 19, 2014.

10. TimelineJS Google spreadsheet template.

11. Capzles, http://www.capzles.com/, accessed December 20, 2014.

12. What is Mind Mapping? (and How to Get Started Immediately), https:// litemind.com/what-is-mind-mapping/, accessed December 20, 2014.

13. Creately, http://creately.com/, accessed December 20, 2014.

14. StatPlanet, http://www.statsilk.com/software/statplanet, accessed December 23, 2014.

15. StatPlanetUser Guide, http://www.statsilk.com/files/resources/User_Guide_StatPlanet.pdf, accessed December 23, 2014.

16. UN Data, http://data.un.org/, accessed December 23, 2014.

17. StatPlanet download, http://www.statsilk.com/files/software/StatPlanet.zip, accessed December 23, 2014.

18. Publishing using DropBox, http://www.statsilk.com/support/faq#dropbox, accessed December 23, 2014.

19. Publishing using Google Sites, http://www.statsilk.com/support/faq#google-sites, accessed December 23, 2014.

20. DataFerrett, http://dataferrett.census.gov/index.html, accessed December 20, 2014.

21. Users Guide, http://dataferrett.census.gov/UserResources/DataFerrett_UserGuide.pdf, accessed December 22, 2014.

22. Tips and Tricks, http://dataferrett.census.gov/UserResources/TipsTricks.html, accessed December 22, 2014.

23. FAQ, http://dataferrett.census.gov/FAQs.html, accessed December 22, 2014.

24. How It Works, http://www.tableausoftware.com/public/how-it-works, accessed December 24, 2014.

25. Training, http://www.tableausoftware.com/public/training, accessed December 24, 2014.

26. FAQ, http://www.tableausoftware.com/public/faq, accessed December 24, 2014.

27. Community, http://www.tableausoftware.com/public/community, accessed December 24, 2014.

28. Gallery, http://www.tableausoftware.com/public/gallery, accessed December 24, 2014.

29. Georgia EPD Brownfields Program, https://epd.georgia.gov/brownfields, accessed December 24, 2014.

30. Mapbox Guides, https://www.mapbox.com/guides/, accessed December 24, 2014.

31. Mapbox Help FAQ, https://www.mapbox.com/help/, accessed December 24, 2014.

6

TIPS AND TRICKS

Every project can be made better with a little inside knowledge or at least a bit of advice from one who has gone before and returned to tell the tale. This is where you get the inside scoop on what works and doesn't work for me when using the tools I have used while writing this book. Just because I liked an online tool a few weeks ago doesn't mean that the developers haven't made changes or tweaks that make me dislike the tool now. The same thing may happen to you on your journey through the world of telling stories with data. Something that works well for me may not be so great for you so remember that your mileage may vary. However, I hope everything here seems like common sense to you.

WHAT TO DO

If you have read a chapter or two of this book you know that the mantra for success is plan, plan, and plan some more. The only way you can plan too much is to spend all of the time allotted on the plan and none on the execution. Planning includes determining what story you want to tell. It also requires figuring out your budget of time and money. Then consider what format will show your story in its best light and choose your tools accordingly. Finally, think about how you want to tell your story and what information you already have available and what pieces you will need to collect, keeping in mind your time budget.

Another what-to-do is to go out and look at the work of others, both professionals and amateurs. This is how you can figure out what you like and don't like and see what tools others are using to do the same work you want to do. The Internet is full of graphics and visualizations just waiting to be seen, so feel free to take a tour and become inspired. Remember that this is a way to learn and not an invitation to copy others' work. Think of it like an art student studying the *Mona Lisa* or *Starry Night* and drawing it to learn technique but not to create an exact replica.

The next what-to-do is to take time to play with the various tools discussed in this book to find out what works well for you, your organization, and the stories you usually tell. If nothing presented here feels right for you, please take the time to search the web and find another tool you do like. This is a hot area and there are hundreds if not thousands of online tools available for creating infographics and data visualizations. They come in all types, at all price points, and for all levels of skill. Feel free to have an adventure just discovering new tools and taking the time to learn them with at least a minimum level of proficiency.

The search for the perfect tool match is best done before you reach a deadline. It is difficult to go hunting for a new tool with a due date looming. If you have already taken the time to figure out what you like in a graphics editor or modeling package before you decide to create something, it will be much easier and far less frustrating for you.

The last big what-to-do is to have fun. Most likely no one made you pick up this book and no one is requiring that you create an infographic about anything. You picked this book up because it looked like fun. Take some time to practice and let your creativity flow before you bust out the knowledge that you can do this cool new thing to your colleagues or your boss. It takes some of the pressure off when someone does ask you to create something fabulous and you know you've already done it.

WHAT NOT TO DO

Please, I beg of you, do not procrastinate. It will make you frustrated as you work with what might be a half-baked idea, perhaps less data than you need, and without an inside knowledge of the tool you have chosen to use. Creating a bad graphic is as bad as, if not worse than, creating none at all when one was expected. Please, don't procrastinate.

Don't decide that an infographic or a data visualization is the best answer in all situations that call for data display. There are many situations where such a graphic would be useful but they are only likely to pop up in a news library, where they still exist. For almost everyone else in library land there will be a limited number of situations where visual presentation using these kinds of tools is the absolute best way to get information from you to the audience. Once you have a brand new hammer it is easy for your mind to only see nails but resist the urge to use all of your shiny new toys where the finished product will not be attractive or easy to read and you may find yourself discouraged from trying again.

Don't lie with data. This is not just a do or don't but really a matter of ethics. If you have data that doesn't say what you want it to say, find out why. Was there an error in data collection? Did you move a decimal point? Is it just really true that the shiny new branch library just built with bond funds and filled with brand-new books and eager staff members only had fourteen reference questions, three computer use sessions, and twenty-three circulations in the first month? If that is the case, you have to put this information in a report, and you have chosen to do it with a data visualization, be sure that what your audience sees is the truth. No matter what, find out what is going on. The eager new staff members seem to have time on their hands, so ask them what's happening and request that they think of ways to market that branch and the great services it offers. If the truth is something closer to the fact that the branch is swamped in patrons, then it's time to find out where that recordkeeping went wrong. By no means is it time to hide anything with a pretty picture. It can be easy to hide data in a three-dimensional model or by manipulating the axes of a graph, but resist the urge. Our ethics as information professionals are important and shouldn't be compromised because some data doesn't look particularly flattering.

Don't feel constrained by the templates provided in the online tools. Almost every one of the products has a completely blank canvas you can start from. Then you can use all of the editing features provided and make something you are proud of. Most also give you the option to upload pictures and other files. Maybe you want to have your school's mascot on an infographic or want to see your company's logo and corporate colors in the background of a data visualization you are making for the marketing department. By choosing the right tools and having the skills to get the files uploaded in the correct format, you are now the master of your graphic. There is no need to let a computer program tell you who's boss when you are the one telling the story.

SOME BEST PRACTICES

There is a fine line between dos and don'ts but I will straddle it by making these best practices somewhat pithier.

Plan.

Take time to be inspired and to look and understand how others have created what you want to create.

Pick the right tool for the job and don't try to cram the right data into the wrong format for visual communication.

Know your story and how you want to tell it.

You know the story you are telling better than anyone else, so feel like the expert as you work.

Don't procrastinate.

Think about color and font before you get started.

Draw a picture, no matter how rough, of what you want your finished product to look like.

If you don't like a tool, don't use it and find something you do like.

Feel free to alter templates, colors, shapes, fonts, or anything else until you get the look you want.

Practice before you need to do this for real.

Get to know the quirks of your favorite tools and any limitations those tools may have, especially when you have a choice between the free and fee version of a tool.

Understand why you are doing this project with these tools and if it doesn't make sense to you, consider finding another way to tell this story.

When you pick a color palette, consider whether you think it just looks nice or if it has some meaning to the story you're telling or to your organization.

Use words sparingly unless there is a good reason to do otherwise.

Label anything that needs a label to give it meaning, like the x and y axes of a chart or graph.

Give yourself enough time to tell your story.

Give yourself permission to mess up and delete your whole graphic if that is what you feel needs to happen.

If you do mess up, take a little time off and start again, remembering that while this might be important, your infographic is not the key to world peace or perfect harmony and is also not the *Mona Lisa*, so cut yourself a little slack.

Relentlessly, constantly have the story you are telling in mind as you work.

Show off what you have done on your webpage, to your patrons, and to your colleagues.

If you can enter your creation for a professional association or other award, do it. Just because an award is for publications doesn't mean that an infographic or a data visualization is out of bounds. Who knows, maybe you'll win. (See chapter 4.)

Have some fun and think of this as something like using finger paints at work.

7

FUTURE TRENDS

DATA VISUALIZATIONS AND INFOGRAPHICS ARE HERE TO STAY

Data visualizations are now firmly a part of our world. The mere fact that *The Best American Infographics of 2013* has been published shows just how common these pictures with a story are in American life. You can find them anywhere from popular websites like Reddit with its Data Is Beautiful[1] section showcasing beautiful, astonishing, or just plain entertaining examples created by amateurs and professionals alike, to Flowing Data, a site devoted to data visualizations and created by Dr. Nathan Yau, author of several well-regarded books on visualization and a dissertation on "personal data collection and how we can use visualization in the everyday context. That expands to more general types of data and visualization and design for a growing audience."[2]

Infographics and visualizations are also tremendously useful. The modern world bombards us with data every day. Much is trivial and entertaining and can be easily dismissed. However, some of this data is vital to us as citizens, voters, and human beings. There is a wonderful book called *How to Lie with Statistics*[3] that was published in 1954, long before all of the tools discussed in this volume were even a twinkle in the eye of a computer scientist or statistician. The chapters include "The Sample with the Built-in Bias," "The Well-Chosen Average," "The Little Figures That Are Not There," "Much Ado about Practically Nothing," "The Gee-Whiz Graph," "The One-Dimensional Picture," "The Semiattached Figure," "Post Hoc Rides Again," "How to Statisticulate," and "How to Talk Back to a Statistic." Any of them could be written today about the ways that graphics and visualizations can be used to skew data points to make them say whatever you want or need them to say in the circumstances. The vast majority of you reading this book mean for your visualizations and infographics to be used as teaching tools or to provide information in a way that is transparent and without agenda. Politicians, pundits, charities, beverage companies, airlines, and more want to use these tools to put themselves or their causes in the best light possible. This might mean using an infographic that doesn't show the full picture that the data paints. It might also mean using odd scales on the axes of a visualization or putting it in three dimensions to conceal data that is less than flattering or shows that the other side might be more correct on an issue than is desired.

As information professionals, our job is to promote information literacy. One of the ways we can do this is by making excellent infographics and data visualizations and showing our patrons how to determine if what they see in the local newspaper, online, on television news, or in a magazine is trustworthy. Just as you take the time to help people learn to tell a trustworthy source from one that isn't so trustworthy, you now have the tools in your hands to help your patrons make better decisions about these ubiquitous images.

DATA VISUALIZATION AND GRAPHIC DESIGN IS A GROWING BUSINESS

With a computer and a little skill anyone can be a graphic designer. Some, however, have turned their expertise into thriving businesses. One of these is Visual.ly. The site acts as a sort of online dating platform for companies or organizations to find a project team of designers, writers, and a project manager to create a custom campaign that can include infographics, presentations, videos, and more to design a tailored brand, all for a price far cheaper than going to a brick-and-mortar design firm. How do they keep the price low? For one, Visual.ly has no building where all of the creatives (industry speak for the designers, writers, programmers, and project managers) show up every day. Instead, the team is made up of freelancers who may not reside in the same country, let alone the same city. They also have the flexibility to put together a team that is just the size and made up of just the skill sets that you need.

As a librarian looking to make a relatively simple infographic, this approach may be overkill, but if your organization was looking to make a large marketing push to raise awareness or drive usage, the base fee of $995 might seem like a great investment. To use the service you never have to leave your desk because all communication is by telephone, Skype, or e-mail. This gives you the time you need to actually run your organization while people with the skills to do branding and marketing are busy making your vision a reality.

Beyond the mostly hands-off approach you take with Visual.ly, consider all of the other tools discussed in this book. With a few exceptions, every tool is created as something you can use for free or as a subscription service, with the fee version giving you many more options of templates, tools, download formats, and screen resolution. These tools are all part of businesses, and these businesses have the mission of every business—to make a profit. Thus the ease of starting to use a tool and then the options that are just out of reach but visible to you until you buy a subscription.

More and more bright, tech-savvy students are graduating from high school and college every year. The economy has changed in such a way that they are unlikely to get traditional jobs where they go to an office every day and complete a forty-hour work week. These graduates are far more likely to join a start-up or maybe start one up themselves. With so many tools for creating visualizations and infographics, any one of them could figure out the next great thing and become the creator of the go-to tool until someone else comes up with an even greater new thing.

As an end user, all of this competition is good for you. It means you can have new and easier-to-use tools while the prices the market will bear must remain somewhat stagnant and may even inch toward the great dream of the Internet, information that wants to be and is free. Perhaps one of you will even join in the fun and create the next great thing as you gain experience making graphics and think "wouldn't it be better if—?"

YOUR AUDIENCE WILL EXPECT THEM

Although it starts to sound a bit like a broken record, infographics and data visualizations are all around us. You can't open a newspaper, flip through a magazine, watch television news, or browse the Internet without coming across some visual representation of data. These representations are an excellent way to share a large amount of information in a bite-sized package. Your patrons, especially those who have grown up in the age of the Internet, will expect to see data presented to them in a visual format, the easier to enjoy on a tablet or smartphone and the better to use on the go than a chart or page of prose.

Members of your audience are busy, whether with school and family responsibilities, job stress, or just about any other list of activities you can imagine. They want to get information quickly and they want to be entertained. An infographic created in bright colors with attractive representations of data fits the bill. Not only will your patrons like to see this style of information transfer; they have come to expect it and will want more of it. You can use this style as a way to reel in non-traditional library users, either to come into the physical library or to use the materials you offer online. Don't think of it as a ploy to be "hip to the young people" but instead consider it a way to share information with anyone. While infographics are definitely a very trendy thing now, they need not all be targeted to and made for teens and young adults. Once you start using these techniques to transfer information about your library, your services, or other interesting topics, you'll find that it is not just the Internet generation that has come to expect them. It will be professors, parents, grandparents, senior partners, and anyone you can think of who has a need or desire to use your particular library. Consider this another way to promote and improve information literacy for the audience you work with most often.

NOTES

1. Data is Beautiful, http://www.reddit.com/r/dataisbeautiful/, accessed December 18, 2014.

2. About, http://flowingdata.com/about/, accessed December 18, 2014.

3. Darrell Huff and Irving Geis, *How to Lie with Statistics* (New York: Norton, 1954).

RECOMMENDED READING

BOOKS

Affelt, Amy. *The Accidental Data Scientist: Big Data Applications and Opportunities for Librarians and Information Professionals*. Medford, NJ: Information Today, 2015. This newly released book is a must for librarians and other information professionals who want to enter the world of Big Data in corporations, law firms, consulting, or anywhere else large collections of data congregate. Affelt explains terms and discusses options for creating value added data in numerous settings.

Beegel, Justin. *Infographics for Dummies*. Hoboken, NJ: Wiley, 2014. *Infographics for Dummies* may seem too simple to include here but it is a very good introduction to tools and techniques, especially techniques for using tools that may already be on your desktop or could be requested for purchase because of the multiple purposes they serve, like Adobe Photoshop and Illustrator.

Cairo, Alberto. *The Functional Art: An Introduction to Information Graphics and Visualization*. Berkeley, CA: New Riders, 2013. With DVD. *The Functional Art* is a textbook of sorts by Alberto Cairo, a professor in the University of Miami's School of Communication. The first two sections discuss why visualizations are useful and the science behind why graphics can be more easily understood than prose. Cairo then provides numerous examples, some in Portuguese, for practice in creating useful infographics and visualizations. The fourth section is a series of profiles of the foremost data designers working today. The included DVD is an expansion of the book and not merely a digital version.

Cook, Gareth, ed. *The Best American Infographics 2013*. New York: Mariner Books, 2013. This book is a must for inspiration, although it does not provide any real guidance on creating your own infographics.

Emerson, John. *Visualizing Information for Advocacy: An Introduction to Information Design*. Berlin, Germany: Tactical Technology Collective, 2008. Available online athttp:// backspace.com/infodesign.pdf, accessed December 24, 2014. This slim booklet is designed to teach nongovernmental organizations (NGOs) and other groups engaged in advocacy how to effectively choose a story to tell and to create beautiful and informative graphics and visualizations to inform the public and educate and persuade lawmakers and others in power about the importance of the issues for which the group advocates.

Evergreen, Stephanie D. H. *Presenting Data Effectively: Communicating Your Findings for Maximum Impact*. Los Angeles: SAGE, 2014. *Presenting Data Effectively* is about all kinds of data, not just what might go into an infographic or data visualization. Evergreen's book is a good resource to have on hand for any presentation needs but also provides ideas on how best to make a page interesting and why some visual representations are superior to others for clarity and style.

Few, Stephen. *Now You See It: Simple Visualization Techniques for Quantitative Analysis*. Oakland, CA: Analytics Press, 2009.*Now You See It* serves to act as a primer on data analysis and visualization and creates a stunning picture of how beautiful and clear visualization is as a tool for communication. The middle section of the book describes major types of data analysis and provides explanations and applications for everything introduced.

———. *Show Me the Numbers: Designing Tables and Graphs to Enlighten*. Burlingame, CA: Analytics Press, 2012. *Show Me the Numbers* is all about creating excellent tables and graphs from very few or very many variables. There is a full section devoted to defining *chart* and *graph* and to understanding the differences and when one is a better vehicle than the other. Few discusses how best to tell stories with numbers and points out the "silly graphs that are best forsaken."

Huff, Darrell, and Irving Geiss. *How to Lie With Statistics*. New York: Norton, 1954. A classic look at how statistics are used and misused to sell products, influence public opinion, and influence decision makers. This short work is an excellent primer on keeping numbers honest for anyone beginning work with statistical modeling and data visualizations.

Kellam, Lynda M. *Numeric Data Services and Sources for the General Reference Librarian*. Oxford, UK: Chandos, 2011. Kellam's slim volume discusses how librarians in any library can collect data for internal and external purposes and work to encourage information literacy. It also provides a comprehensive listing and description of data sources available online as well as some data visualization resources. Each chapter is meticulously footnoted and includes a bibliography along with a selected annotated bibliography. Perhaps the most interesting part of the book is a listing of the librarians interviewed with their comments and descriptions of their various library types.

Krum, Randy. *Cool Infographics: Effective Communication With Data Visualization and Design*. Indianapolis, IN: Wiley, 2014. *Cool Infographics* discusses the whys and hows of the form from the perspective of a professional infographic designer. Krum discusses why infographics are so appealing, how to use interactive features in online graphics, and how to design graphics for maximum effect and appropriate data usage.

Lankow, Jason, Josh Ritchie, and Ross Crooks. *Infographics: The Power of Visual Storytelling*. Hoboken, NJ: Wiley, 2012. This book covers much of the same ground as the other books in this list, including cognition, visual storytelling, formats, and tools. Where it shines is in the selection of images to illustrate the book, often page after beautiful page at a time. *Infographics* includes great information that is organized well, but it may be most useful as a book of inspiration from beautiful and creative examples.

LeFever, Lee. *The Art of Explanation: Making Your Ideas, Products, and Services Easier to Understand*. Hoboken, NJ: Wiley, 2013. *The Art of Explanation* is geared to business marketing. It also is a book about telling stories and choosing the right medium for the message while explaining how to work within the time, cost, and materials constraints common to all enterprises.

Meirelles, Isabel. *Design for Information*. Beverly, MA: Rockport, 2013. *Design for Information* is a series of case studies showing gorgeous examples of graphics and visualizations arranged by theme. Meirelles intersperses discussions of history and best practice throughout the book.

Smiciklas, Mark. *The Power of Infographics: Using Pictures to Communicate and Connect with Your Audiences*. Indianapolis, IN: Que, 2012. *The Power of Infographics* is a straightforward guide to using infographics, particularly in the business marketing sense. The book includes a very nice chapter on the ROI (return on investment) of using infographics and a chapter of resources including shapes and pictures to try, types of charts, graphs, and diagrams, tools for creating your own graphics, an annotated further reading section, and an annotated list of some of the many design firms and freelance designers who are creating infographics now.

Tufte, Edward R. *The Visual Display of Quantitative Information*. Cheshire, CT: Graphics Press, 1983. A true classic, one of four books clearly laying out what to do and what to avoid when telling stories visually.

———. *Envisioning Information*. Cheshire, CT: Graphics Press, 1990. A true classic, one of four books clearly laying out what to do and what to avoid when telling stories visually.

———. *Visual Explanations: Images and Quantities, Evidence and Narrative*. Cheshire, CT: Graphics Press, 1997. A true classic, one of four books clearly laying out what to do and what to avoid when telling stories visually.

———. *Beautiful Evidence*. Cheshire, CT: Graphics Press, 2006. A true classic, one of four books clearly laying out what to do and what to avoid when telling stories visually.

Walter, Ekaterina, and Jessica Gioglio. *The Power of Visual Storytelling: How to Use Visuals, Videos, and Social Media to Market Your Brand*. New York: McGraw Hill Professional, 2014. *The Power of Visual Storytelling* is truly a marketing book, but the importance of marketing should not be lost on information professionals who have customers as surely as a store, a bank, or any other business. The opening chapters on storytelling as a tool are probably the most relevant to the use of graphics and visualizations in library settings.

Wong, Dona M. *The Wall Street Journal Guide to Information Graphics: The Dos and Don'ts of Presenting Data, Facts, and Figures*. New York: Norton, 2010. Wong's book is an excellent reference for the use of color, font, and types of graphics. It includes a short section on keeping those who are colorblind in mind when using color as the differentiator between indicators. The book also includes a section on the math to remember when using data and describes what to do with data that is less than perfect. This slim volume is a reference tool any visualizer would be wise to have at hand.

Yau, Nathan. *Visualize This: The FlowingData Guide to Design, Visualization, and Statistics*. Indianapolis, IN: Wiley, 2011. *Visualize This* provides a thorough introduction to all aspects of data visualization. It includes explanations of terms commonly used by data scientists, helpful hints for creating visualizations, and a broad array of tools from simple and free to complex and expensive. The book is an excellent next step for going further with visualizations.

———. *Data Points: Visualization that Means Something*. Indianapolis, IN: Wiley, 2013. *Data Points* is Yau's follow-up to *Visualize This* where he explains how not to create visualizations and how to do it correctly. Yau discusses important points like issues that may exist in your data, how to present data to people, and using legends and annotations to bring clarity to data. This book is highly recommended.

PRESENTATIONS

Kelleher, Christa. *Communicating through Infographics: Visualizing Scientific and Engineering Information*, presented by the Special Libraries Association Transportation Librarians Roundtable (TLR) and sponsored by IEEE. July 10, 2014, slides and archived presentation available athttp://ntl.bts.gov/networking/tlrarchive/201407/index.html, accessed December 24, 2014.

Phelps, Marcy. *More Than Pretty Pictures: A Guide to Data Visualization for Info Pros*. Phelps Research, presented by the Special Libraries Association Leadership and Management Division, September 10, 2014, slides and other materials available athttp://www.phelpsresearch.com/Speaking, accessed December 24, 2014.

WEBSITES

Backspace, http://backspace.com, accessed December 24, 2014.

Chart Porn, http://chartporn.org/, accessed December 24, 2014.

Cool Infographics, http://www.coolinfographics.com/, accessed December 24, 2014.

Data Store, http://www.theguardian.com/data, accessed December 24, 2014.

Data Visualization, http://apandre.wordpress.com/, accessed December 24, 2014.

FlowingData, www.flowingdata.com, accessed December 24, 2014.

Information Aesthetics, http://infosthetics.com/, accessed December 24, 2014.

Information Is Beautiful, http://www.informationisbeautiful.net/, accessed December 24, 2014.

Many Eyes, http://www-01.ibm.com/software/analytics/many-eyes/, accessed December 24, 2014.

9 Captivating Data Visualization Projects, http://mashable.com/2012/10/04/data-visualization/, accessed December 24, 2014.

10 Fascinating Data Visualization Projects, http://mashable.com/2013/03/05/data-visualization-projects/, accessed December 24, 2014.

Visual Complexity, http://www.visualcomplexity.com/vc/, accessed December 24, 2014.

Visualising Data, http://www.visualisingdata.com/, accessed December 24, 2014.

Visualizing, www.visualizing.org, accessed December 24, 2014.

BLOG POSTS

Duarte, Nancy. "The Quick and Dirty on Data Visualization," *HBR Blog Network*, April 16, 2014, http://blogs.hbr.org/2014/04/the-quick-and-dirty-on-data-visualization/, accessed December 24, 2014.

Parikh, Ravi. "How to Lie with Data Visualization," *Heap's Data Blog*, April 14, 2014, http://data.heapanalytics.com/how-to-lie-with-data-visualization/, accessed December 24, 2014.

Ricks, Rebecca. "5 Next Steps for Data Visualization," *Domosphere*, May 29, 2014, http://www.domo.com/blog/2014/05/5-next-steps-for-data-visualization/, accessed December 24, 2014.

INDEX

ABOUT THE AUTHOR

Sarah K. C. Mauldin is a law librarian in Atlanta, Georgia. She spent a short time as a public librarian in Austin, Texas, before beginning her law firm career in Las Vegas, Nevada. She is deeply involved in library professional associations, including the American Association of Law Libraries (AALL) and its Private Law Libraries, Reference Instruction and Patron Services, and Legal Information Services to the Public special interest sections and its Atlanta and Southeastern chapters; the Special Libraries Association (SLA) and its Leadership and Management and Legal divisions and Georgia chapter; and the Georgia Library Association (GLA). She has served in various capacities in all of these organizations, from committee member and chair to board member to president. She was the inaugural recipient of the AALL Emerging Leader Award in 2010 and is a frequent speaker and writer on issues related to technology in libraries, law librarianship, and access to justice. Sarah is also an active community volunteer with projects including the AJC/Decatur Book Festival and the Decatur Martin Luther King, Jr. Service Project and serves as Board Secretary for 7 Stages Theatre. She is a 2013 graduate of Leadership DeKalb and continues to volunteer with the program. In her spare time she enjoys trivia, euro board games, Sooner sports, and almost any fiber art. Sarah holds a B.A. in Letters from the University of Oklahoma and an M.L.I.S. with specialization in Law Librarianship from the University of Texas at Austin. She lives in Atlanta with her husband Ryan and two marvelous orange cats.